# KIDS EXPLORE
# KIDS WHO MAKE A DIFFERENCE

*Westridge Young Writers Workshop*

John Muir Publications
Santa Fe, New Mexico

*This book is dedicated to child bonded laborers*

John Muir Publications, P.O. Box 613, Santa Fe, NM  87504

Printed in the United States of America
First edition. First printing June 1997

**Library of Congress Cataloging-in-Publication Data**
Kids explore kids who make a difference/Westridge Young Writers
  Workshop.
           p.      cm.
     Includes index.
     Summary: Features young people who have made a difference in their
own lives and in the lives of those around them.
     ISBN 1-56261-354-5
     1. Child volunteers—Juvenile literature.  2. Young volunteers—
Juvenile literature.  3. Heroes—Juvenile literature.
   4. Children's writings, American.  [1. Voluntarism.  2. Heroes.
   3. Children's writings.]  I. Westridge Young Writers Workshop.
HQ784.V64K53 1997
302'.14—dc21                                         97-5616
                                                       CIP
                                                       AC

**Editors:** Chris Hayhurst, Lizann Flatt
**Graphics Coordinator:** Mladen Baudrand
**Production:** Marie Vigil, Nikki Rooker
**Design:** Susan Surprise
**Typesetter:** Marcie Pottern
**Printer:** Publishers Press

Distributed to the book trade by
Publishers Group West
Emeryville, California

# CONTENTS

# ACKNOWLEDGMENTS

The authors and teachers wish to graciously thank the following people and organizations for their contributions to this book:

❖ Columbine Elementary School
❖ Deer Creek Middle School
❖ Nancy Gilder of the Mayor's Commission on Youth
❖ The Giraffe Project and especially A. T. Birmingham-Young
❖ Jennifer Gilligan of the Points of Light Foundation
❖ Julie Meeks of Volunteers of America

❖ Karen Hirshfield of Reebok
❖ Peiffer Elementary School
❖ Prospect Valley Elementary School
❖ Ronald G. Adams and Broad Meadows Middle School
❖ Wilma Soloman of the Association of Jewish Family and Children's Agencies
❖ Wilmore Davis Elementary School
❖ Westridge Elementary School and especially Debra Murphy and Lisa Skidmore
❖ 9 News Kids Who Care and Diana Sotelo

And a very special thanks to the parents of all the heroes and the authors. Thanks to moms and dads, all our work is possible!

# STUDENTS' PREFACE

Have you ever thought you could make a difference in our world even though you're a kid? We're here to tell you that you can. Our purpose for writing this book is to share with you some of the young people in the world today who are reaching out to make a difference. We think they are heroes. These young people have done exciting things to help themselves and others. They've helped the homeless, the sick, the elderly, the environment, and other kids and people. These kids are not like Superman. They don't have super powers or the ability to fly. They are not the kind of people who would run into a burning building to save a life. Instead, they are super kids who are willing to help whenever and wherever they can.

We have learned that heroes are everyday people who live in the world around us. We believe the best heroes are the people who have made a commitment to make our world a better place. We have learned that no matter how young you are, where you live, or what you do, the effort that you put forth can change things. Some of our heroes volunteer to help others, some speak up for human rights, and others organize events to help those who are less fortunate. They are honest, kind, caring, and helpful. They try to do things the best way they can. They have helped in big and little ways. They stick up for their beliefs, but they don't put other people down. If there's a problem, heroes try to help as much as they can to fix the problem. They don't give up on the goals that they have set. They don't make problems for others to solve; they're in the solution business.

All of the heroes we met have made a difference in their own lives, too. We think that is just as important as helping others. We believe we all have to be strong inside ourselves to make our world a better place. This is one way a hero earns respect from others. All our heroes know helping themselves and helping others go hand in hand. We hope you find, as we did, that helping others not only strengthens the hearts of the people you work with, but your own heart as well.

This book was written for kids by kids, but that doesn't mean adults can't read it too. No matter how old you are, you'll probably find this book fascinating. Read these stories and learn from them. It was fun learning about these people and writing about them. Finding the heroes around you isn't hard and you can show them that you like what they're doing. We hope you enjoy reading about these young people and we hope you like the chapter Getting Involved. Just like these kids, you may discover that you too can make a big difference.

# TEACHERS' PREFACE

Adults often complain that young people have the wrong ideas about who they value as heroes. Maybe kids get the wrong ideas because they often define a hero as someone who is famous, far away, and almost invariably older than themselves. These myths can create vast distances between kids and their genuine desire to do something heroic. With this book, teachers hope to bridge that gap and empower young readers to pursue the numerous heroic opportunities available to them daily. As these young heroes exemplify, everyone can make a difference in our world.

This book, the seventh book written by the Westridge Young Writers Workshop, is a compilation of profiles written by children under the direction of classroom teachers. Indeed, these authors are heroes themselves, because through their hard work and valiant efforts, the message "kids can make a difference" rings true on every page.

The young heroes profiled in this book are from cities across the nation and were found through local and national organizations and by word of mouth. Their stories were compiled, processed, and reviewed by the teachers and authors, with careful attention given to the facts that were most meaningful to young readers. The teachers served as guides and consultants, while the students devoured the research and processed the manuscript. Special consideration was given to the writing, editing, and polishing of the text. Thus, both the writing process and the subject matter were equally important to the final product.

As the writers learned how these heroes have used their talents to help others, many of them were inspired to do the same. With just a little effort, they have discovered that they can be more like the people they admire. Besides hoping to improve themselves, the authors have expressed their desire to see other young people become interested in creating positive changes.

We, the teachers, hope to encourage you to seek out local and national heroes of all ages to bring into your own classroom studies. Find them! Research them! Interview them! Write about them! Draw them! Photograph them! The study of heroes within the classroom is an appropriate and alluring topic to create truly meaningful discovery among students of all ages. A highly versatile theme, heroes can be examined alone or in relation to subjects ranging from literature to social studies, science to music, politics to physical education. Our heroes invite us to explore and appreciate one another like nothing else we'll ever teach or study. Truly, the best heroes teach something to everyone, and their stories have a lasting impact on the lives of the people who explore them. Often overlooked, heroes are one of our nation's greatest treasures.

# JIM STUART RUNNER-BEUNING

*Achiever and Inventor*

The countdown started. Ten, nine, eight, seven, six, five—it was about to happen. The *Atlantis* was going to take off. Four, three, two, one . . . ORROOM! The space shuttle blasted off! Fire was flaming out of the shuttle. The air was filled with smoke and flames. It went up, up, and up. Jim Stuart Runner-Beuning was glued to the TV, watching the space shuttle launch and listening carefully. He knew something special, something of his, was on that shuttle. He watched the silver rocket go off into space with his own tree seeds from Alaska on it. The shuttle kept getting smaller and smaller until it disappeared, then nothing was left but a trail of smoke.

That had been a special day for Jim Stuart Runner-Beuning. He was very excited to see his own stuff go up in space. He remembered when he was ten years old and he became involved with an incredible NASA (National Aeronautics and Space Administration) experiment.

Jim had heard about some tomato seeds that had gone up in space and he had sent a letter to NASA asking about them. They sent him some of the seeds. After Jim planted the seeds, he kept track of them. He planted some normal tomatoes for comparison. He discovered that the space tomatoes grew differently. They grew every which way, and the tomatoes were in bunches instead of being spread apart.

Jim also experimented with the tree seeds that were sent into space on the

Runner-Beuning family

*Jim is excited about biology and more.*

*Atlantis.* Jim had gotten involved with this experiment through his local 4-H club. NASA had been looking for volunteers to grow the tree seeds, so Jim decided to try that, too. After the space shuttle landed, NASA sent the seeds back to Alaska, where Jim lived. These trees grew the same way as the tomatoes had grown—strangely. The needles were yellow-green and bright green instead of their usual color. Today these trees are grown in national landmarks, open areas, and on the grounds of the White House in Washington, DC. Jim also sent some of the trees to Russia and Japan

for goodwill. Jim has made a commitment to NASA to watch and study these special trees for the rest of his life.

Jim's seeds aren't his only contribution to science. Jim has been involved with the Arctic Science Conference since he was in the sixth grade. This conference is a meeting of many scientists who come together to share ideas about the Arctic region. They invited Jim to the conference because he had made up his own interesting research projects. The scientists felt they could learn some new things from Jim. Even though he is much younger than the scientists, Jim has given a total of six presentations at the Arctic Science Conference through the years.

In 1994, Jim began an internship at the Steward Research Station in Kasitsna Bay in Alaska. This research station is part of NASA and the University of Alaska at Fairbanks. At the station, Jim and the scientists study marine biology. In 1996, Jim became a research assistant, helping even more scientists learn about ocean life. They've been taking core samples of the

ocean bottom, and they're learning about seal populations. Jim is learning more at the University of Alaska at Fairbanks while he's still a high school senior and an honor student. He feels it is very important for him to learn with people his own age.

Jim was born on May 2, 1978, and today he lives in Fairbanks, Alaska. Jim's family is really caring, and they're always thinking about others. His mother's name is Marsha. His stepdad's name is Virgil. Jim has learned how to be a caring person from them. His stepdad owns his own truck. He helps to build roads, and he hauls fuel all over Alaska. His mother has always cared for people of all ages. She has shown Jim how to be a good volunteer and how to help other people. She is legally blind now, so Jim has been able to give her back some of the caring she has always shown to him. Jim also has a godsister named Wing Yan. She's from Hong Kong, and Jim loves her a lot.

When Jim was very young, an important event helped to shape his future. Jim and his mother were all packed to move to Alaska from California. There had been nonstop rain, which caused a mudslide in the canyon where they lived. As mud and giant redwood trees hit their house, their home was destroyed. All their possessions were ruined. Even though they felt sadness, they were thankful that they were alive.

Jim and his mom heard that others had lost their lives and homes. Jim begged his mom to take him to a shelter so he could see the homeless people. When they got to the shelter, Jim started running around from person to person. He put his arms around them to give them comfort.

He kept telling them that everything would be okay. A little girl was shivering with cold, and Jim took off his jacket and gave it to her. People were amazed and very thankful to him for making them feel better. This is when Jim got his nickname, Jim the Roadrunner.

Jim has helped many people. He and his mother have purchased clothes and coats for many needy people in Alaska. They have made many trips to the local thrift stores to buy coats for others. They stored the coats on racks in their garage. The coats came in different sizes. Jim and his mom washed them and then fixed them by sewing buttons, zippers, and tears. Then they gave them away to people who needed coats. Jim hopes the coats will help the needy people stay warm in the cold of Alaska.

Jim has continued to think about other people. He has raised chickens, ducks, and geese for people in need. He has helped clean up the environment. One day, in seven hours, Jim picked up 65 giant garbage bags full of trash all by himself. He has taught bicycle safety and fixed up old bikes just like new to give to needy kids. He learned CPR so he could help save people's lives. He volunteers all the time, and it could never be any other way for Jim. Helping others is his way of life.

For a time in his life, Jim experienced being handicapped. Because of this, he became more understanding of others with special needs. Jim was in the third grade when he began to have problems with his feet. He had a hard time walking. The doctors at the Shriner's Hospital said they could help him. They made him a brace to go under each foot. The braces would help his feet grow into the right shape. The braces had a funny name, "cookies." Most cookies taste good, but not the ones Jim had to wear!

When Jim was 16, his feet were corrected, and he didn't have to wear the cookies anymore. The Shriners called Jim the "Miracle Child" because his feet healed so quickly. Whenever anything bad happens, Jim has always told himself, "I need to put my past behind me and look to the future." Jim knows that he can't change the past, but he can try to make the future brighter. As the years have gone by, this attitude has helped him.

Even the cookies never kept Jim from his favorite sport, track and field. When he would run in races with his cookies on, he

*Jim has a wall full of awards and honors.*

Runner-Beuning family

would tell the kids with disabilities that he was running for them. Jim would share the medals and ribbons that he had won with them. He still likes to compete and do the long jump and the hurdles. Jim has competed in the Native Youth Olympics (NYO) and the World Eskimo Indian Olympics (WEO). In the WEO, men and boys of all ages compete with each other in all kinds of sporting events. Even though Jim wasn't as big as many of the men in the competition, he won a bronze medal in a very hard event called "drop the bomb."

Lee is one special friend that Jim met at the Native Youth Olympics. Lee wanted to go to college. Jim helped Lee get elected as the top sportsman and best athlete. Then, Lee earned a scholarship for his encouragement and training of youth in sports. Lee and Jim are thankful to have each other as friends.

Jim has always tried to make new friends. All of his friends are very special to him no matter how old or young they are. Jim has his own golden rule, and he believes we should all follow it: Keep old friends as gold and new friends as silver to become gold in time.

Chip is another one of Jim's best friends. He's the same age as Jim. They have a lot in common. Even though they go to different schools, they like to spend time together. They both like to volunteer, go mountain biking, and work on special computer programs. They love to talk and share ideas.

Another of Jim's special friends is an older man named John. John let Jim in on a secret about cutting gems, especially turquoise. John shared this secret with only one person, and that was Jim. John trusted Jim not to tell anyone because they were such good friends.

Jim continued to be interested in rocks and gems. One day when he and his mom were driving in the car, Jim asked if she could stop so that he could go rock hunting. His mom stopped the car and

*Jim designed a warm scarf named Roadrunner Thermo-Weave.*

watched him hunt for rocks. Jim came running back to the car with two unusual rocks. Jim showed his mom the rough and bumpy rocks, with brown, red, orange, and white marks on them. Some parts of the rocks looked almost like glass. The two rocks weren't very pretty. His mom figured they were ordinary rocks, but Jim knew that they weren't. The rocks were so unfamiliar that Jim decided to take one specimen to a scientist.

The scientists didn't know for sure what the rock was, but some thought it might be a meteorite. It turned out that no one had ever found rocks like these. They are so rare that one of the rocks has been displayed in a museum. The rock that Jim has is kept in a safety deposit box in a bank so that it will be protected. These rocks have been named after Jim and are called Jimite. Jim should feel very proud of himself for making this discovery.

Over the years, Jim has enjoyed learning many things from older people. One of Jim's favorite places to volunteer has been at senior citizen centers. He has gotten to know a lot of people and he has made many older friends at a variety of centers. Jim always brings them baked goods, crafts, cards, squeezy balls, or posters he has made. Many of the seniors are old bush pilots, and they have told Jim stories about flying in Alaska. He says that the old are wise. Jim is interested in doing things with his hands, and the seniors have taught him new things like crocheting.

Jim used his skill at crocheting to help one of his favorite teachers who had playground duty. When it got cold outside, Jim decided to crochet her a scarf. He stayed up all night working on it. He made the scarf with a different kind of crochet stitch. After he made the first scarf, word spread around about how warm and comfortable it was. Jim taught many other people his special crocheting. Soon the design was nicknamed Roadrunner Thermo-Weave. These scarves have become famous across Alaska and other places too.

Jim is a very creative and artistic person in other ways, too. Jim's creative writing and photography have won several awards through the national PTA (Parent-Teacher Association) Reflections Contest. This is a contest that you can enter at your own school. Jim also collects Aleut, Alaskan

Cuckoo

Indian, Eskimo, and Native American art. He likes to make a lot of native art projects. Many of his handmade projects have won grand prizes. Jim also fixes all kinds of clocks. His house is full of grandfather clocks and lots of cuckoo clocks.

Jim has lots of other interests and hobbies. He has made many different kinds of model airplanes. He made a model helicopter and a P51 Mustang fighter plane. He's also made a British SE 5A. This is a big plane that is radio controlled and can fly 80 miles per hour. Jim really enjoys this hobby with his dad. They discuss the models and fly them together.

Jim and his mom also have a huge rubber stamp collection. They have thousands of stamps stored in wooden drawers. Some of the stamps make noise when you use them. They have cartoon stamps, Elvis stamps, and many more. Jim uses the stamps to make cards for people who have done something special and for people who need to be cheered up.

Jim also enjoys caring for his six pets.

He has a sheltie dog whose name is Sparky, four hamsters, and a bird that likes to eat with the family. The bird, Candy, also likes to perch on the hamster cage and watch them play. All these hobbies give Jim a lot of pleasure.

Since 1991, with the help of his neighbors, his mom, and his dad, Jim has made many squeezy balls. A squeezy ball is one balloon filled with rice with two more layers of balloons over it. These squeezy balls help people with hand problems. People can relax or exercise their hands and reduce their stress by playing with them. Jim and his parents and neighbors worked on the balls in Jim's kitchen for hours. Jim used many bags of rice and thousands of balloons. There was rice all over the place. At one time, his family had bought every 9-inch balloon in the city of Fairbanks!

The balloon project got quite expensive, but Jim said it was worth it. He was contacted by a university about this project, and he has written and published a paper to tell about the squeezy balls. He has also

given lectures about them so that more people can be helped.

We learned how to make the squeezy balls in our fourth grade class, and we shared this activity with other classes. After we finished, some kids traded the balls. We all had fun playing with them. The best part was making something that our hero had made.

Jim has accomplished many things, but the thing he is the most proud of is Kids Who Care. In 1989, Jim had an idea for getting other kids involved in volunteering, so he started a program called Kids Who Care. It is a program set up for youths all over the world to get started in volunteering. He believes the world would be a better place if everyone learned to help one another.

The Voice of America radio program heard about Jim and the project. They talked about it on the radio, and within 35 days the program spread around the world. Lots of people became interested in Kids Who Care, and children all over the world began to volunteer.

Jim made thousands of certificates by hand for the people who completed their volunteering. He used his stamp collection and hand embossed each one. He personally wrote each volunteer's name on every certificate. After a while the project got to be too expensive for Jim. He started asking people in groups like the PTA, girl scouts, boy scouts, and churches to run this program on their own. Today these and other organizations are running their own Kids Who Care programs, and the organization is still a national success.

In fact, we started a Kids Who Care program in our school. Some of us played with the younger kids in our neighborhood or helped an older person take care of his or her yard. It has been a lot of fun and many of us are enjoying volunteering for the first time. Our teacher gave each one of us a special certificate. You could start this program in your school, too.

Jim knows that volunteering is a wonderful thing to do. He hopes that when the people he has helped get better, they will also become volunteers. Jim is a great person and has taught us to think about others before ourselves. He even volunteers some of his time teaching English as a second language. He likes talking to people who speak other languages, so he's also learning Japanese, Chinese, and Korean.

Jim has received more than 100 awards since he was very young. He was the

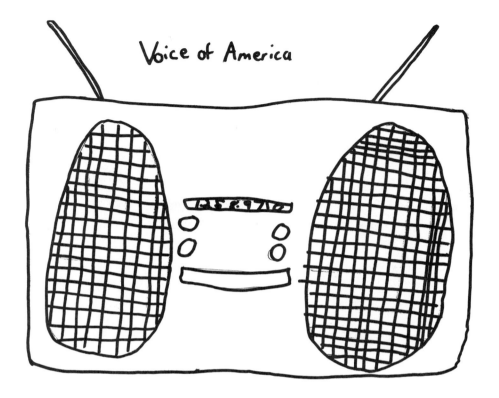

first youth to receive the Jefferson Award and the New Generation 7 Who Care Award. He has been on television. He has received letters from presidents, governors, senators, and NASA congratulating him on his work.

Someday, we know Jim will achieve his dream of inventing a new field of study. He'll call this new field Integrated Robotics. He wants to design robots that will help people in everything from archeology to paleontology to medicine. This way, he'll get to keep learning about and participating in all the things that he's always been interested in. It's not every day that we meet a hero like Jim.

## Here is a letter from Jim:

*It was an honor, privilege, and pleasure to work with the enthusiastic and talented Westridge Young Writers group . . . .*

*There are three basic concepts that I would like to share with you that have helped to shape my life, and I would hope they could be advantageous to you.*

*First, you are the result of how you perceive the events that happen to you and how you handle them. Everyone has to face problems and events they would like to avoid. Try to handle them in a thoughtful, caring, and positive manner. Think of the obstacles, problems, and even temporary failures as learning experiences of the past. The present is now, and the future is yet to come. Make the present and the future bright! Volunteering helps to show the positive way you deal with others through your sincere caring.*

*Second, get the best education that you can. Make that special effort to do your best. Remember, the more you learn, the more you will be able to help yourself as well as those around you . . . . Learning is a lifelong adventure which promotes a positive attitude about life and understanding others. Again, your volunteer skills will be enhanced along with leadership skills.*

*Third, you must feel good about yourself and stay drug free . . . . Take your favorite talent (we all have one or more), and use it to help others. You will have so much fun helping in that first project that you will look forward to other projects. . . . The size of the project is not what is important, it is your dedication, caring, and enthusiasm that counts. The more you volunteer, the more you will want to continue to help others. You can make this a better world through your own individualized volunteering. Go for it! Have fun volunteering!*

# CARI RONS
## *Courageous Kid Helping Herself*

Sometimes you can't tell a kid is a hero just by looking at her. Sometimes a hero can be just like the kid next door. It can be a kid who had a difficult time when she was a baby, but still hasn't given up trying. It can be a kid who tries to help others by telling them about what she's been through. It can even be a kid who makes a promise to herself to always have a better life. We know a kid just like that. Her name is Cari Rons.

When Cari was born on April 10, 1983, she weighed only 4½ pounds, even though she was two weeks overdue. Most babies that are overdue are heavier, but Cari's mother was taking drugs and drinking while she was pregnant. This is very

bad for babies. Then things just kept getting worse for Cari.

When Cari was a baby, her four-year-old sister had to take care of her and her brother when their mother went out to bars. Finally, when Cari was two years old, her uncle called the police. When the police came to get Cari, they found her lying in her crib all dirty. She wasn't changed or cleaned up. Just imagine being left all alone for a long time with dirty diapers and only another kid to take care of you. This is called child neglect, and it's against the law for parents to do that to their children.

Cari and her brother were taken away from their mother and adopted by new parents who could take better care of them. They went to different families so

Rons family

*Cari's dad, her dog, Buster, and another dog join her while camping.*

a few small words. She also has ADD (attention deficit disorder) and other learning disabilities.

Right away, Cari's new parents started getting her into many kinds of therapy to help her catch up to other kids. She learned how to show emotions by acting out *Snow White and the Seven Dwarves* and nursery rhymes like "Little Miss Muffet." Cari also has a dog named Buster who is a special part of her therapy. Cari is learning to take care of Buster so she will know how to care for others. Buster is Cari's best friend. Making friends has always been hard for Cari because other kids have thought she is too different.

Even though making friends and learning new things is hard for Cari, she still wants to learn things that other kids can do. One time, she really wanted to learn how to turn a cartwheel, but her body just wouldn't do what her brain wanted. Cari didn't give up. She kept trying and finally she learned. She was so excited about it that she practiced outside, at the park and playgrounds, in the halls, at the mall, and even on the way to bed! When she wanted to get somewhere, Cari would cartwheel. Cari learned how to cartwheel so well that by the time she was in her seventh grade gym class, she was one of just a few kids who could do lots of cartwheels in a row. This is just one example of how important learning new things has been to Cari.

Now Cari goes to a public school in Littleton, Colorado, where she's involved in activities like the writing club and the chess club. She told us that she wants

they could get lots of extra attention to make up for what they had missed. Duane and Dixie are Cari's parents now, and she has an older brother named Nathan.

Cari has had many problems to overcome. For one thing, she had to get used to a whole new family. Besides this, Cari wasn't acting and learning like most children. No one knew exactly what was wrong with her. Because she was not hugged or kissed, she also had problems understanding emotions. She didn't have any tears or facial expressions. She had very little muscle control, and she couldn't walk well. She's had problems with her speech and hearing, and she could only say other people to hear her story so they will know how bad it is for pregnant mothers to drink and take drugs. Cari never wants others to go through what she has been through. Even though Cari has had many challenges in life, she still never gives up and she believes in herself.

We think it would take a lot of courage to be like Cari because she has had so many difficult things to overcome. We think people can help mostly themselves and still be heroes. If people help themselves, they help the whole world. They can set an example for others to follow. Cari has shown her courage by proving that even if people have many challenges, they should never give up. By doing this, Cari shares her courage with everyone.

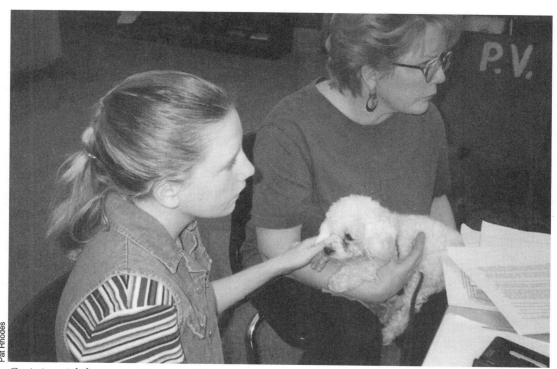

Pat Rhodes

*Cari sits with her mom, Dixie, and Buster.*

# TEDDY ANDREWS
## *Young Politician*

Have you ever thought of being president of the United States? Seems like an impossible dream? Well, not for Teddy Andrews. No, he's not the president yet, but give him time. Teddy has spent almost his entire life in politics. Think we're exaggerating? Guess again. Teddy has already been appointed to one governmental position, and he's worked with many other people who were running for office. He is also the youngest member of the California Democratic Party. Sound pretty cool? What's really cool is that Teddy was only seven years old when he became a government official. Yes, that's right, seven years old.

It all started back when Teddy's mom decided that part of his homeschooling should be spent learning about politics. Teddy had been homeschooled since he started his education. A tutor came to his house five days a week. Just imagine being the only kid in your class and not getting to talk to any classmates or play at recess! This didn't bother Teddy because he got to study lots of things he liked and, by the time he was seven years old, he was doing high school work. He studied geometry, algebra, physics, and paleontology, which is the study of dinosaurs. He even learned to speak some Chinese. Teddy was learning loads of stuff.

Teddy was doing so well in school that his mom wanted him to get out and use his intelligence to help others. At first, Teddy didn't give a hoot about politics, but his mom started taking him to meetings

St. Mark's Preparatory School

*Teddy Andrews in 1996*

anyway. Teddy was sometimes embarrassed to be in a room full of adults. But, Teddy soon decided it wasn't so bad. He was interested in helping the homeless and so was Don Jelinek, who was running for City Council. Teddy decided to campaign for Mr. Jelinek. He ran errands, handed out literature, and put up posters. Some of the people in the area where Teddy was campaigning spoke Chinese, so Teddy spoke to them in Chinese. At first it was scary going door-to-door talking to people, but Teddy got used to it.

Teddy was excited when Don Jelinek was elected to the City Council. He decided to ask Mr. Jelinek if he would appoint him to the Berkeley Youth Commission. Even though it was called a youth commission, there had never been a child

on it before. Mr. Jelinek thought it was time for a change so he appointed Teddy to serve on the commission. This made Teddy Andrews the youngest appointed U.S. official in history.

Because it was so unusual for such a young boy to be doing so much, Teddy was invited to be on the *Tonight Show* with Johnny Carson. It was a very strange visit for Teddy. He was very honest with every question he was asked on the show. One of the first questions Mr. Carson asked was if Teddy liked the show. Teddy replied, "I really have never seen your show, except for once. My grandma wanted me to be on your show so I decided to watch it. I saw the episode when your fly was open!" Then Johnny said he had heard that Teddy didn't really want to be on the *Tonight Show,* so Teddy told him why. He said, "Well, when your fly was open, everyone was laughing at you, so I thought people might laugh at me, too."

Teddy has spoken out to encourage others to help the community become a better place to live. He helped create a wish list program by putting together a list of things that homeless families could use, then finding people in the community to provide them. He also helped emcee the Children's Housing Now rally with Geraldo Rivera. He really worked hard to get things for homeless families, especially homeless children.

Teddy's work for his community didn't stop after his official duties as a youth commissioner ended. He then started a group called SAY-YAY (Save American Youth-Youth Activists for Youth).

By starting this group, Teddy helped many kids find ways they could help in the community. This group told the community about things kids need, like food, clothing, and toys. The group convinced the community to open up and share from their heart. It also worked to get the kids in the community involved. Teddy and the group did many things for all kinds of people, including an Easter egg hunt. It was exciting for Teddy to see so many people have such a good time. The group also put on other special events, like canned food drives, clothing drives, and toy drives during the holidays.

Teddy and his actions have received lots of attention. One day Teddy opened up the newspaper and looked. There he found a picture of his friend Kiran Bragg and himself. Wow! What an honor to be seen on the front page of the *Berkeley Voice*. The short but sweet article right below told of his wonderful charity drive where they sold raffle tickets and collected toys, toys, and more toys! He read about how the toy

drive was for kids in the hospitals and the poor. Teddy was really excited, but soon he calmed down and called Kiran. The two laughed and cheered about the article.

Many people have thought Teddy has done a lot. Teddy was given the Giraffe Award for "sticking his neck out" to help others. With that award came another very special honor. In 1990 Ben and Jerry's ice cream company helped sponsor a special event through the Giraffe Project. It was a tour of the United Soviet Socialist Republic (USSR). They picked kids who had worked hard for their community to go on a friendship tour to the USSR. Teddy was picked to go in the summer of 1990. He was so excited. He was only nine years old, and he was the youngest kid picked to go.

Teddy remembers the butterflies he had in his stomach as he got on the plane with the other kids to fly to the USSR. It was a ten-hour flight from the United States. At the beginning of the flight, he enjoyed exploring the plane. As he looked around the plane, he saw that everyone else on the tour was at least three years older than he was. He felt excited but a little worried and scared. The flight went on and on and finally he got some sleep even though he could hear the plane engine the whole time.

When he woke up, the steward told them the plane would be landing soon. It wasn't long before the plane door opened. He was amazed at what he saw. There was a large group waiting to greet the young friendship ambassadors. His eyes kept looking around. He had never imagined the USSR like this, because he had only seen it in books and films.

The next ten days were like a fantasy. There was so much to do and so much to see! There were many new foods to try and

many new people to meet. When he boarded the plane to fly back to the United States, he was sad he had to leave his newfound friends, but he was also happy about going back to his family and friends in the United States.

Teddy has done a lot more in his life than just political and social activism. Since he took his school lessons by himself, he met most of his friends at a neighborhood recreation center. He was on a swim team there for several years. He likes to read, play video games, and watch TV. He has also been an intern for the American Friends Service Committee, and he helped them set up their computer web page.

Teddy decided that he wanted to attend St. Mark's Preparatory School in Southborough, Massachusetts. They gave him an academic scholarship because of his outstanding work. Now he lives there in the dorm and he goes to school with his new friends. He's on the honor roll, and he likes to participate in the school's theater program. We think Teddy might be the president of the United States someday. We know we would vote for him.

### Teddy shared this message with us:

*The young people in our country need to work to change things. To deny one American child health care, food, housing, and an education is called child abuse. To deny 10 million American children health care, food, housing, and an education is called balancing the budget. Why must U.S. youth dine out at dumpsters and sleep at the "Sidewalk Ritz?"*

# RENATA BRADFORD
## *Cancer Survivor Reaches Out*

When you first meet Renata Bradford you probably won't notice how pretty she is. You probably won't see how bright her smile is. You might even miss the twinkle in her big blue eyes. What most people notice is her hair, or rather, her lack of hair. We hope that after you read this story you will look beyond the outside differences in people. We hope that you will look for the beauty underneath and not stop at what you see on the outside.

Renata was born in New Jersey, but when she was four, her family moved to Colorado. She considers Colorado her home because this is the only home she remembers. Her life in Colorado was pretty normal. She had lots of friends, enjoyed

school, and also did a lot of extracurricular activities. She was involved with karate, school volunteer clubs, and, most of all, Westernaires. Westernaires is almost like a school drill team where students dance with flags using a lot of marching steps. But in Westernaires the kids ride around on horses. Sometimes they carry flags, too.

Westernaires was very important to Renata. This program takes a lot of practice because there are a lot of girls and a lot of horses that need to learn the steps. There are many people involved with taking care of the horses and training them. The Westernaires go to performances all over the United States. One time Renata went to Virginia, and all her Westernaires friends and horses went along. They had to drive with the horses in trailers, and they had to

Westridge Young Writers Workshop

*Renata lost her hair because of chemotherapy treatments.*

be very careful with them because traveling is hard on horses. Renata said that one time her teammate had her horse in its stall after a long trip. The horse was so nervous it jumped over the four-foot stall door, and they had to go and catch the horse in a field nearby. Renata told us there's never a dull moment in Westernaires. She always looked forward to the time she spent with her group.

Everything was pretty normal for Renata until she was 14 and she started feeling sick like she had the flu. She went to doctors several times, and they said she just had the flu and that she would get better. One day she threw up so much that her parents took her to Children's Hospital Emergency Room, where doctors took some blood tests. Renata remembers a short little elflike man who told her that she had leukemia, a form of cancer. At the time she had no idea what leukemia was, so she thought that it was no big deal. She

remembers saying to herself, "Give me my pills and let me get back to my life." She wanted to get her problem quickly taken care of so she could get back to her friends and her horses. She realized it was very serious when the doctor told her she might have to quit Westernaires. Renata was devastated and refused to quit. Instead, she took a leave of absence. She said that one of the things that kept her going through her illness and a bad situation was Westernaires. She saw cancer as something she had to get through to get back to her daily life. She told the doctors that cancer wasn't going to stop her.

Soon after she found out that she had cancer, she started getting chemotherapy. Chemotherapy is a chemical treatment that kills cells, such as cancer cells, that grow fast. Hair cells are also fast-growing cells, which is why people who have chemotherapy lose their hair. Chemotherapy includes a toxin, a poisonous substance, that is given to the patient by injection. During chemotherapy patients throw up a lot because their bodies are trying to get rid of the poisonous stuff. Doctors are very careful to watch the amount of chemicals they put into a patient's body, so the chemicals don't cause any permanent damage. The type of cancer a patient has determines how much chemotherapy is needed. Radiation therapy is another treatment used to treat cancer. It is like chemotherapy, only harder on your body. It is given to the patient by lengthy exposure to x rays. Renata went through eight months of chemotherapy and radiation therapy before she was better. That period of time was very hard on her.

Renata told us that every time she had a radiation treatment, as soon as she recovered, she went straight to Westernaires and practiced. One time, right after her radiation treatment, she went to the stock show for a performance. She found a cot there and slept for a couple hours to rest up after the treatment, then her friends helped her get dressed and put her on her horse. She was still very sick, but she went ahead and performed anyway. She had a really good time performing, but after the performance was done she went back and fell asleep on the cot again. She really laughs at this story now and wonders how she ever did it.

At the end of her treatments, the doctors tested Renata and said her cancer was in remission. This means that the cancer had gone away for awhile. Her parents and her doctors knew that if the cancer came back, Renata would need a bone marrow transplant and more chemotherapy. A bone marrow transplant is a way of taking out the cancer cells in bone marrow and replacing them with healthy cells. The bone marrow is where your blood cells are reproduced, so it is very important that the cells come from healthy tissue. They knew it would be hard to find a donor, so Renata's mom asked the doctor if they could freeze some of Renata's own healthy bone marrow in case the cancer ever came back.

The doctor agreed and that summer Renata went to Seattle for her operation. During the operation, the doctors put six holes in her hip bone to get the bone marrow out. Renata said, "It hurt, but the pain went away quickly. My back was sore, but two days later I was back in Colorado riding my horse." Renata's family was thankful that they had saved some of Renata's bone marrow. This meant that if she needed the transplant and they couldn't find a donor, the doctors could use her own bone marrow.

Just before Christmas, the leukemia reappeared in Renata's central nervous

system. The next month, Renata and her dad went back to Seattle. This time they were there for months of chemotherapy, plus the process of transplanting the stored bone marrow.

Renata has many stories about her hospital stays. One time, after a treatment, it was hard for Renata to stand or walk. She was unable to use the bathroom so the nurse gave her a bedpan to use. When she was feeling better she decided that she wanted to try to use the bathroom. The nurse checked Renata's blood pressure and said she should take deep breaths while she was walking. When she got to the bathroom and sat down, she got so excited that she forgot to take deep breaths and she fainted. This was very embarrassing to her. Renata has learned to laugh at good and bad times, and she laughed when she told us this story.

Renata and her dad spent many months at Seattle's Swedish Hospital. If Bill Bradford, Renata's dad, wasn't with her, he was in the cancer ward's family room, where he compared notes with other parents and kept track of other patients.

"You have to be strong," Renata's father said. "You have to feel they're going to survive, and make sure everyone else has that positive attitude. Renata had it. We all had it."

On June 5, 1990, Renata and her father returned to Colorado, exhausted. The cancer was gone and Renata was well, but she was very weak. Renata didn't like being weak because it scared her. One time, when she was alone, she heard a noise in the backyard. It really frightened her because she was so weak that she couldn't even run if she needed to. This was when Renata realized she was really out of shape. She didn't like that feeling at all, so she decided to go back to another favorite activity of hers, karate.

Renata had first started karate when she was in the sixth grade. A friend had invited her to try it and she loved it. She couldn't wait to start her own lessons. Karate taught her to focus and follow through on tasks. When she got cancer, she quit going to karate class because she was too weak. Renata decided that even though she was still very weak, karate would be good for her. She was also feeling really self-conscious because the chemotherapy had left her with almost no hair. She has only a few short, almost invisible wisps of blonde hair left. Before the cancer she had been a normal kid with everything ahead of her, but after the last chemotherapy session and the loss of her hair, she was not very sure of herself. She wasn't used to people staring at her. Some people treated her differently after she got cancer.

Back in karate, Renata got her mind off her problems and the cancer. She made new friends, learned to accept the way others felt about her, and felt better about herself. She told us about the time her instructor asked the young women why they had to tie their hair back for practice. Renata quickly raised her hand, even though she was bald, and said, "So it stays out of your face." Everyone laughed. It gave Renata confidence to be able to make fun of her baldness among friends. Renata tells a lot of funny bald jokes.

Now Renata has her second-degree black belt. She has been a karate instructor and she's been a judge at tournaments. She said that many of the people she judges are better than she is. Renata also said that in karate some people bring home big trophies, but even if you don't bring home a trophy, you're still a winner because you tried.

Another thing that helped Renata get back into her normal life was volunteering. She had started volunteering in high school with the Key Club. This is a group of kids who spend time helping others. It is part of the Kiwanis group, in which adults plan things to help the people in their communities. Renata's club would go to places where elderly people lived and plan bingo games and activities for them. Another thing Renata and the other members liked doing was running the Special Olympics at a school for disabled children. This was like a big field day event, only they gave out lots of awards like they do at the Olympics.

After her illness, volunteering seemed even more important to Renata. When she was in the hospital, her friends, family, and people she hardly knew gave so much to her that she felt a need to give back to others. Renata is good at volunteering because she knows how it feels to be different. Renata loves horses so much that she decided to teach disabled kids how to ride. When she is with the kids, she makes them feel like they don't have a disability and that they can do anything. She also skis in Vail, Colorado, with kids who have been dealing with cancer. When the kids are on skis, they leave all their troubles behind them. They have taught her that anytime she has a problem, she and her family can solve it together.

One of Renata's favorite places to help is at a camp for kids who have had cancer. She has been a counselor and makes camp fun for them. Renata and the other counselors don't make the kids talk about their cancer, but if the kids want to, they will listen. She feels good when she goes there because no one judges her or any of the kids by the way they look or act. Some of the activities that the kids and counselors do are archery, crafts, capture the flag, hiking, canoeing, fishing, and more. They also get their faces painted. One of the counselors is really good at face painting and painted a dragon all over Renata's head. It looked really cool, so each year that same person comes up with something new to paint on Renata's head. Everyone is always excited to see what cool design Renata will wear next.

One of the fun things Renata does at the camp is sit around campfires and tell stories and eat yummy things. Her favorite food at camp is Banana Boats. Here is how you make them:

## Banana Boat Recipe

You will need a banana, some chocolate syrup, marshmallows, and a piece of foil big enough to wrap around the unpeeled banana.

*Directions:*

1. Leave the banana in its peel.
2. Cut the banana in half the long way.
3. Put the chocolate syrup and marshmallows inside the banana peel with the banana.
4. Carefully wrap the banana in the foil.
5. Let it cook on the fire for 5–10 minutes. Be careful when you pull it out. Don't burn yourself.
6. Let it sit to cool off, then chow down.

Renata had a few crazy experiences as a counselor at the camp for sick kids, but this story might be her craziest. One night Renata was in a deep sleep. Her fellow counselor, who happened to be awake for some reason, heard a loud, spooky, crackling noise. She shivered with fright and woke Renata up from a deep sleep. The strange, spooky noises kept getting louder, and this time Renata heard them. Then a sudden gust of wind ran through the trees and the two girls were terrified. They laid there, paralyzed from fear, trying to figure out what the howling noises were. Whoosh! A sensation came over the whole tent as the door flung open. Eeehhh!

Renata and her friend grabbed each other and screamed so loud they woke up the whole camp. Then they looked up and saw it was just another counselor who had been to the bathroom. It was the joke of the camp for many days.

Renata feels good about the time she spends at camp. It is very relaxing, and since all the kids there have had cancer, nobody worries about it. She feels this camp is a wonderful place because all of the kids and counselors respect themselves and the others around them.

When people ask Renata why she does so much to help others, she tells them a story that one of her college professors told her: There once was a girl who was walking along the beach, picking up starfish and throwing them back into the ocean. She was doing this so the starfish wouldn't die. They had been left on the beach when the tide went out and they couldn't make it back on their own. While she was doing this, a man walked up to her and asked her why she was throwing the starfish into the sea. He pointed out to her that there were so many starfish along the beach that even if she worked all day she could not make a difference. After he said this, she picked up a starfish and threw it into the sea. Then she turned to the man and said, "It made a difference to that starfish."

This story shows that everyone is important, and that if everyone worked as hard as that girl did, it would make a big difference. She says that when you see or meet someone who looks different or is having trouble going through a door or something, just stop and ask them if you can help. Sometimes they may just sneer or say no, but you will feel good knowing that you offered help. The job doesn't have to be a huge, tough one. Any help you offer is helping someone and that's what counts.

Renata learned an important lesson when she was sick. She learned that you must be able to accept help as well as give it. When Renata was so sick in the hospital, there were tons of people offering their help. She needed help with getting well and with school. If she hadn't taken the help, a lot of things would not have been done. If you see someone who has nothing to do and you have a whole load of things to do, ask them for help. Give and take—it's as simple as that.

One thing that is still difficult for Renata is her lack of hair. For most people, their hair grows back in just a few months. It has been six years since Renata lost her hair and it hasn't grown back. The doctors think that her hair has not grown back yet because of all the radiation therapy they used on her. She told us, "It doesn't matter if I don't have hair because I'm alive and enjoying life."

Although Renata is getting back to a normal life, she has had to adjust to many things. Renata feels sad when people on her college campus see her coming and either stare at her or look away. She just wants people to treat her the same as they treat other people. Renata's advice to us is that if you see somebody who is different you should act normal so they don't feel bad. Just look them in the eye and smile. Remember, it's the inside of you that counts.

Renata feels very lucky to be alive. She has fought her cancer and she is winning. Renata is still in remission from her cancer, and she is one of the 40 percent of people who survive this type of leukemia. Every year, Renata celebrates the day that she left

*Renata talks to young people about her struggles and goals.*

cancer behind. She and her family have celebrated it for more than six years. The more years she celebrates, the better chance she has of not getting it again. She has found a lot of new friends and, with the support of her family and friends, she is getting out there and enjoying life.

## Here is a letter from Renata:

*These are a few of the most important things that I've learned in the first couple decades of my life:*

- *There is no set purpose in life except the one you create for yourself.*
- *The way you look at the world determines what the world looks like.*
- *Without pain and sorrow, we would have no appreciation for the wonders of love and joy.*

    *There is no such thing as a life without challenges, and some challenges are harder to overcome than others. In any case, challenges*

*look a lot smaller when you've got people around you who care and who are willing to help you.*

    *My own personal experiences have led me to a desire to help other people whenever and wherever I can. . . . But I also realize that I need to take care of my own needs, such as taking care of my health and achieving personal goals.*

    *Helping people makes me feel good, and very often I get a better perspective on my own problems when I help others deal with theirs. It's very easy to get stressed out or depressed over little things, but when I see the problems that other people deal with, or even when I look at my own life and what I've already achieved against the odds, I can see what really is important, at least to me: the companionship of family and friends, the beauty of the planet we live on, and a sense of humor to soften the blows that life all too often deals us. . . .*

    *I wish you all the best luck in navigating the twists and turns of life!*

# ASHLEY BLACK
*Activist Against Hatred*

The first prime minister of Israel, Golda Meir, once said, "Nothing in life just happens. It isn't enough to believe in something. You have to have the stamina to meet obstacles and overcome them—to struggle." Golda Meir would be proud of Ashley Black. She has the stamina to meet obstacles, and she takes action to change them.

One night when Ashley was ten years old, she watched a very upsetting news report about Nazi video games. She could not believe her eyes and ears. The reporter told how Nazi video games were being played in Europe. The point of the games was to put Jews or Turks in concentration camps and kill them. In one of the awful games, players pretend they are the commandants of a camp. They sell slave labor, gold fillings taken out of dead people's teeth, and lampshades made from the skin of corpses to get money to buy gas chambers and poisonous gas. Ashley Black felt sick after listening to this news story. She told her family that she didn't think people should make a profit from other people's tragedies. Ashley liked to play video games herself, but felt they should be fun and educational. They should not teach hate, racism, or prejudice. That night, Ashley decided she had to do something to stop these games from coming into New Jersey where she lives.

Ashley decided to write a petition and get people to sign it. A petition is a kind of letter to the government, signed by lots of people who are concerned about something.

Black family

*Ashley in 1996*

She felt a petition would make the government see that many people were upset about these games. Part of the petition read, "Computer games that allow the player to act as the commandant of a Nazi concentration camp and oversee the hanging of inmates are not games and must be stopped. If we all join together, we can fight against the evil people who are having fun with the terrible tragedies of the Holocaust." Ashley asked her younger brother, Jeremy, who was eight, to help her collect signatures. Jeremy and Ashley got 500 people to sign their petition. After Ashley and Jeremy told other people about the problem, they too volunteered to pass around

copies of the petition. The group worked hard and even got the attention of the news media. Although it sometimes made Ashley nervous, she did her best to make people understand the problem. She even spoke at a press conference and told others about the situation. In just two weeks, more than 2,000 people signed their names on the petition.

Because she worked so hard, Ashley got to meet with lawmakers to convince them to write bills and laws to stop these games from being sold in New Jersey. Once again Ashley had to tell her story to get the lawmakers interested in making a change. Her hard work and the support of a lot of people helped get two bills written and made into laws. Two New Jersey legislators, George Spadoro from Middletown and Neil M. Cohen from Union, sponsored the legislation, which banned the possession of video games that promote hatred of people based on their race, color, religion, or ethnic origin. Today, people in New Jersey who are caught with these video games have to learn about the Holocaust, pay a big fine, and go to jail for up to 18 months.

Ashley has won many awards and has done many special things. She was the first winner of the Reebok Human Rights Youth in Action Award with a $5,000 scholarship. This award was created because of what she had done at such a young age and the great example she has set for people of all ages. At the awards ceremony, Ashley got to meet former U.S. President Jimmy Carter and other famous people who were involved in helping others. Because Ashley "stuck her neck out," she was honored as a Giraffe by the Giraffe Project. Ashley was also surprised when she was awarded the Woman of Influence Award at her local Jewish community center. The publicity didn't stop with awards. She was on TV shows like *Nick News*, *The Arsenio Hall Show*, *CBS Morning News*, MTV's *The Week in Rock*, and "Face the Hate and Answering Children's Questions about Prejudice" with Peter Jennings.

Ashley's work to make our country a better place hasn't stopped. Ashley enjoys helping her community in many ways. She is vice president of the Community Service Committee in her Jewish youth group, and she volunteers at a hospital. She likes to

visit people in the hospital and cheer them up. She told us her work doesn't only cheer up the patients, but it also makes her happy to see their smiles and to know she is helping. She tutors people who are learning English as a second language. She's spoken in a seminar at a local college. She is on the Board of Advisors of the Andrew Goodman Foundation. Andrew Goodman, a Jewish man, died 30 years ago in Mississippi. He worked with other civil rights activists who were trying to get equal rights for all people. This committee recognizes and celebrates anyone who wants liberty and justice for all.

Even though this makes Ashley sound like a star, she's pretty much just a regular kid like you. She was born in Brooklyn, New York, on November 21, 1980. Her family moved to a suburb in New Jersey when she was four. She lives with her parents, Marlene and Andrew, and her younger brother, Jeremy. Her family means the whole world to her, and she told us that Jeremy is her best friend. Ashley believes she has her parents to thank for her success because they have always supported her and her brother 100 percent. They have taught her that any time she has a problem, she and her family can solve it together.

Since Ashley's family is not together during the day, they try to eat dinner together every night and talk about the day. Dinner time at the Blacks' house is always a special time with many laughs. It's also the time that the family discusses any problems they have and makes plans. Ashley plans to attend college and she's looking around for the best one.

Black family

*Ashley met former president Jimmy Carter at an awards ceremony.*

Black family

*Marlene, Jeremy, Ashley, and Andrew Black enjoy a Florida vacation.*

Ashley and her family enjoy celebrating holidays together. Ashley's favorite religious holiday is Passover and her favorite American holiday is Thanksgiving. Another thing Ashley likes to do is go to the museums, shops, and parks in Manhattan, a part of New York City. She likes the city a lot because everyone is different and unique. No matter where she goes, she sees many different kinds of people. Ashley is not afraid to be herself because she thinks it would be boring if everyone were the same.

Ashley isn't always doing political stuff. She works very hard at school and is a good student. She loves in-line skating. She loves to go fast and feel the wind blow through her hair. She loves playing with her two dogs, a miniature poodle and a golden retriever, because she thinks it's funny to see a big and a little dog play together. Ashley likes to sing, dance, and act. Each summer she goes to a sleep-away theater camp. She says it is great to meet new people and she has fun doing performances and practicing her acting skills. In the summer of 1997, Ashley will go to Israel for six weeks. She is very excited about it.

We know Ashley Black has the strength to help make the world a better place. We hope that her story will encourage you to take a stand for what you believe in, too.

### Ashley gave us this message:

*Always remember, you can make a difference no matter how old you are. If you believe strongly enough in something, the possibilities are endless. Do not get discouraged if you feel you are too young to take a stand. When you are younger, you will not only get a group of young people listening to you, adults will listen too. We, the children, are the future, and we are needed to help make this world a safe, better place.*

# IQBAL MASIH
*Child Laborer Inspires Others*

It may surprise you to know that there are still many people in the world today, including children, who are slaves. The only difference is their masters don't call them slaves. They call them bonded laborers.

Bonded labor is like slavery because the person is sold like a slave and must work off the money to go free. The person must work hard nearly every day for up to 14 hours a day. If the person refuses to work, they'll be beaten. A lot of the child slaves get beaten for things they did accidentally and for being sick. Some kids are even held in chains. Many have to pay for their mistakes by working extra years at a factory.

When Iqbal Masih was four years old, his parents sold him into bonded labor at a carpet factory in Pakistan. The carpet factories need little children because it is easy for them to tie the little knots in the carpets. Children can also be talked into doing hard work because they are young and they don't know any better. Many children in Pakistan are also eager to make money for their poor families. Iqbal's parents owed a lender about as much as 12 American dollars, but they didn't have any money. This is a big debt in Pakistan, and there was no other way for his parents to pay the money except to sell Iqbal. They didn't know things would turn out so badly for him.

Like the other child slaves, Iqbal was treated terribly. Six days a week, he worked

Reebok

*Iqbal led the fight to free children from bonded labor.*

up to 14 hours a day. He never got to play or act like a kid. He was often yelled at, harassed, beaten, and tortured. Sometimes he was even chained to his carpet loom so he couldn't run away. If he was given food at all, it was only about a handful of rice a day. Because Iqbal wasn't fed well and he had to sit or crouch at his loom all day, he hardly grew at all. After six years of hard labor, Iqbal was ten years old, but he was just about the size of a five-year-old kid. Iqbal only dreamed of being free and going to school.

When he was ten, Iqbal and some other kids from the factory snuck out of their prison. They went to a freedom day celebration that was held by the Bonded Labor Liberation Front (BLLF). At the gathering, a speaker told the crowd that no one has the right to own another person. When he heard this, Iqbal realized they were talking about him. He learned child slavery is actually against the law in Pakistan, but many carpet factory owners are community leaders, so they're never punished.

Iqbal was so inspired by what he heard at the rally that he gave a speech to the audience about his hard life. After that, he refused to go back to the factory. Then Iqbal got a lawyer through the BLLF who gave him a letter of freedom. When he showed this letter to the factory owner, he freed himself.

After he was freed, Iqbal began to achieve his dreams. He went to a school for children who were bonded laborers. He decided he wanted to become a lawyer so he could help fight against child slavery. He also wanted to build a school for other freed children so they could learn just like he'd been doing.

Iqbal really wanted to help the other children in Pakistan so he also started speaking out against child labor. He gave many speeches and he led marches in front of factories where children were enslaved. This was dangerous because child labor has made some important people in Pakistan a lot richer. But Iqbal was determined to help stop child slavery. His efforts helped to free thousands of other illegally bonded child slaves.

The shoe company Reebok heard about Iqbal's heroic efforts. They decided to give him the Reebok Youth in Action Award for his bravery. When Iqbal went to the United States to collect his award, he wanted to go to an American school to see what it was like. So, on December 2, 1994, Iqbal went to Broad Meadows Middle School in Quincy, Massachusetts. While he was at the school, he spoke to Ron Adams' class of seventh-grade students.

With the help of a translator, he told the seventh graders about the child labor problem in Pakistan, where more than 7 million children are illegally enslaved. The Quincy kids were shocked by the stories Iqbal told them about his life in the carpet factory. Iqbal also shared his dream about one day building a school in Pakistan for freed bonded children. The Quincy kids wanted to do something to help kids like Iqbal in Pakistan. They just weren't quite sure yet how to help.

Iqbal returned home to Pakistan, his life at school, and his public speaking against child labor. Then a very sad thing happened. On Easter Sunday in 1995, Iqbal was riding his bike along the street near his grandmother's house. On that day, somebody shot and killed him. People knew Iqbal had been murdered, but the police never arrested his killer.

The Quincy kids found out about Iqbal's murder, and they were very upset. We think it is very sad, too. We know Iqbal was a hero because he spoke out for what he believed in, even though it was dangerous. He was kind and he wanted to help others. He didn't want them to suffer what he had been through.

Iqbal was so courageous and his dream was so strong that it didn't fade away when he died. The Quincy kids have carried on Iqbal Masih's hope in a very special way. If you read the next chapter, you can learn all about their hard work to keep Iqbal's dream alive.

# IQBAL'S FRIENDS IN QUINCY
*Kids Helping Other Kids*

If you read the last chapter, you learned the story of young Iqbal Masih's sad life. Remember the kids Iqbal visited at Broad Meadows Middle School? Iqbal really touched their lives. Kelly Mullen said, "I never knew about bonded labor before. It makes me feel lucky to live in the United States." Another student named Robert Dilks said, "I learned today that on the other side of the world there are kids like us, but they don't live the same life we do."

The Quincy kids still remember how Iqbal looked when he came to their class. When they first saw him, they knew something was wrong. They remember being amazed that a person their age could be so small. He was small because he'd been starved most of his life, and he didn't get to exercise and play outside. When he sat in one of their chairs, his feet didn't even touch the ground. They remember the horror story he told them of his life. James Zeng said, "I think no one should have to live his story." They remember the scars he showed them from all the beatings he was given. Another student, named Dan Long, said, "I asked him if he was beaten at all. He said he couldn't even count how many times he was hit." They also learned that millions of kids in other countries are slaves. They were so sad to learn that so many other kids were treated just like Iqbal, they decided to take a stand against child slavery.

Right after Iqbal went back to Pakistan, the Quincy kids found the names

Ronald Adams

*Students at Broad Meadows Middle School wanted to continue Iqbal's work.*

and phone numbers of carpet stores that carried rugs made in Pakistan. They called carpet stores and asked them not to carry rugs that were made by child slaves. Most of the store owners insulted them, but a few understood and said they wouldn't carry these rugs anymore. The Quincy kids wrote hundreds of letters to newspapers and politicians, and they wrote to Iqbal's country pleading for change. They also wrote to other countries, like India, the Philippines, and Morocco, where millions more children are bonded laborers. Their teacher, Ron Adams, helped them out along the way.

When the Quincy kids heard the news that Iqbal had been murdered, they were saddened and devastated. They all gathered at their school even though it was during their spring break. They mourned his death together. Some cried and some just hugged each other. They were all terribly upset. They had a small memorial service for Iqbal. Then they put all their sadness into more hard work.

The kids decided they wanted to do something big in memory of Iqbal. They knew Iqbal's dream had been to build a school for child slaves who had been freed. They decided to build that school for Iqbal. They e-mailed other schools, asking for money to build a school in Pakistan. They asked for donations of $12. Twelve was the dollar amount that Iqbal was sold for, and 12 was his age when he died. Then they set up a web page titled "A Bullet Can't Kill a Dream. Help Keep Iqbal's Dream Alive." They did this to raise public awareness about child slavery, and they asked people to make $12 donations. The web page made their campaign spread throughout the whole world. Two of the students, Amanda Loos and Amy Papile, even spoke to members of Congress to tell them about Iqbal and about their campaign.

All of the Quincy kids' hard work has really paid off. Altogether, they've raised about $130,000 to build Iqbal's school. This is so much money that they can not only build the school, but also keep it going for three years. Some of the money will also buy back 50 kids who are in bonded labor.(To contact the School for Iqbal Fund, look for the address in the Resource Guide of this book). The Quincy kids have even won awards from Reebok and the Giraffe Project.

All along the way, the Quincy kids had some tough decisions to make. One hard decision was who would build the school? They decided to use a construction company that wasn't part of the Pakistani government. When they tried to find a place to build the one-room schoolhouse, they found out that boys and girls in Pakistan could not be together in the same classroom. They decided to build a two-room school so boys and girls could both get an education.

Soon there will be a school in Pakistan for Iqbal. It is being constructed near the border of India in the city of Kasur. That is about 55 miles south of Iqbal's hometown of Lahour. It will be a school for kids who are four to twelve years old. About 200 students will attend. The school will try to reach children already in bonded labor or at risk of becoming slaves.

We think Iqbal would be happy to know that a new school will soon be built in Pakistan. We think he would also be proud of the Quincy kids and all their campaigning. Iqbal helped the Quincy kids believe they could change a terrible thing, even on the other side of the world. As Amanda Loos said, "I feel now like it is my responsibility to make a difference. I feel like I want to do everything I can to help Iqbal and all the other carpet children." The Quincy kids have shown the whole world what a difference a bunch of dedicated kids can make.

# BRIANNE SCHWANTES
*Sharing Her Strengths with Others*

Brianne Schwantes is 15 years old and lives in Milwaukee, Wisconsin. She's happy, confident, and funny. She encourages others to go for it. Brianne stands out in a crowd and fights for what she believes in. She says it feels great to help others. She gathers supplies for flood victims, testifies in front of the United States Senate and committees of the House of Representatives, and gives speeches around the country to educate people about her rare disease. Because of all the things she has done, she has had many special things happen to her. She has met presidents of the United States and was even blessed by Pope John Paul II.

Brianne has osteogenesis imperfecta (OI), which is sometimes called brittle bone disease. Her bones are very fragile, weak, and brittle, and they break easily. It's a dangerous condition because she can't run or even pull very hard, so Brianne has to be very careful to not get hit or bumped. But that doesn't stop her.

Osteogenesis imperfecta is very unusual. The effects of OI start while a baby's body is being formed in its mother's womb. The doctors don't know what causes it. They believe it is the result of a problem with the genes in a person's body. It is a very rare disorder and not many people have it. Brianne is the first patient with OI to be studied by doctors through his or her entire life. Many doctors study her case history when treating other patients with OI. The doctors don't have a cure. They do know that physical therapy, exercise, and

*Because of her bone disease, Brianne is much smaller than most teenagers.*

Jennifer is 5 feet, 8 inches tall. Brianne told us that she might be shorter but she is still older.

Brianne has had many surgeries to help her body. Soon she will have surgery on her jaw. Brianne's jaw is very weak, and it is hard for her to chew some of her food. Although it is a serious surgery, Brianne is pretty excited because the doctors are also going to work on the rest of her face. She is quick to say that her face really doesn't look bad, but that some parts grew more than others. When the doctors go to fix her jaw they are going to even out her other features. She laughs because she wanted them to make her look like one of the supermodels, but instead they are going to make her look more like her sister.

Brianne has learned to make the best of her life, and she tries to help others understand that people with OI are not that different. She prepares and gives many speeches for the National Institute of Health (NIH). This is a major department in the United States government that has programs for people with OI and other medical problems. Almost every time there is a new president or a new budget, Brianne goes to bat for the NIH. She gives speeches in front of Congress. She talks to the budget committees that help decide how much money goes to each special program. These programs include developing new treatments or finding a cure for OI.

walking helps to make an OI patient's body stronger.

Brianne takes good care of her body. She has to keep her bones and muscles strong by watching what she eats and exercising. Her favorite exercise is swimming. Because Brianne's bones can break easily, she has already broken bones in her body more than 300 times! She actually broke 13 bones before she was born. She can break a rib just by hiccupping. Since Brianne has lived with this situation all her life she doesn't notice the pain much anymore when she breaks a bone. Brianne is not as tall as other kids her age because OI also causes her bones to not grow as well. She is only 4 feet, 5 inches tall. Her friend

Before speeches, Brianne gets very nervous. She spends about one week preparing her speeches and about one day arguing with her dad about what sounds best. Most of her speeches are about herself

Schwantes family

and osteogenesis imperfecta. While she's giving her speeches, she feels like she is very powerful because the adults she is speaking to pay so much attention to her. After all, she's just a teenager and every one of the senators and representatives are hanging on every word she says. It leaves her very awestruck.

Brianne also gives speeches to educate people all over the United States. She speaks to Rotary Clubs, Lions Clubs, Optimist Clubs, and school groups. She tells her life story and what it is like to have a rare disease. She feels that the more people know about OI, the more comfortable they'll feel around people with it. By getting out there and sharing her story, she also encourages others to do their best. She shows them that although it can be hard for her, she still gets out and helps people.

Along with giving speeches all over, Brianne and Megan, a friend who also has OI, write a newsletter for kids and families

of kids with OI. Megan lives in Pennsylvania. The girls have worked together to make *Little Bones*, a quarterly newsletter. Brianne and Megan started *Little Bones* because they felt that other kids who have the disease feel different and need a place to share their feelings.

In order to put the newsletter together, Brianne talked to her friends and family and many other people. She also talked to Megan about what the newsletter should look like and how to put it together. Since they live so far apart, most of the newsletter is done by computer. Brianne even has a fax machine at her house and they are always sending things back and forth. They also communicate with e-mail on the Internet. Many of their ideas come from family and friends, plus they have an address where anybody can send information or ask for information on specific things. The girls feel it's important to let anyone send in stuff for the newsletter.

That way they know that they are answering other people's questions. If you would like to contribute to Brianne's newsletter or find out more about *Little Bones,* you can send an e-mail message to terrysch@execpc. com.

The newsletter also addresses the different problems that kids with OI have. It gives ideas on where to buy clothes that are cool and come in smaller sizes. In one issue it explained how to make pantyhose that are way too big fit just right. The newsletter gives ideas on how people with OI can participate in sports. The girls admit that OI kids may not be major-league players, but they encourage them to give sports a try. Because they know how different OI kids feel and how hard it is to find someone else who can understand, Brianne and Megan will set up pen pals through their newsletter.

Megan and Brianne aren't the only people who write for the newsletter. There

are movie, book, and CD reviews sent in by friends and other people who read the newsletter. Brianne's sister, Lizzie, helps with "SIBS," a column for siblings of people who have OI. It's an advice column. Kids write in with questions about their brothers and sisters with OI and Lizzie gives advice on how to handle things. Brianne and Megan enjoy this newsletter and hope to keep it going for many years.

Brianne has won lots of awards. Her favorite is the gold medal she won for her science fair project. In her project she compared the sense of smell and the sense of taste. We think that her other awards are important too. When Brianne started kindergarten, she was sent to a special school for kids who had learning disabilities. The school district thought that since she was in a wheelchair she would have trouble learning. Her parents knew Brianne didn't need to go to this special school. They fought to get her into a regular school. Her parents even took the case to court and won. Brianne now goes to a regular school. She did so well there that the Council of Administrators of Special Education (CASE) gave Brianne the CASE Award.

Another award that Brianne has earned is the Yes I Can Award. Brianne went to Denver, Colorado, to get it. She met Neil Smith of the Kansas City Chiefs football team. It was a lot of fun. Neil Smith was very tall. Brianne said it was hard to imagine just how big a football player is until you meet one in person. The award goes to children who do a lot of community service. Later, a mission used

Schwantes family

*Megan and Brianne got together to create* Little Bones.

Brianne's story in their fundraising brochure. With Brianne's support, they were able to raise more than $20,000 for an orphanage in South Africa.

Brianne has been doing community service for most of her life. She says that when she was born she needed a lot of extra help and her family and community was there for her. She feels like she wants to do as much as possible for her community to give them back what they gave to her. One of the most amazing things Brianne did was to help in Iowa after the bad floods. She knew the people would need clothes, medical supplies, cleaning supplies, and food. She wanted to help get these things to them. Brianne had to really talk her parents and doctors into letting her help. They were afraid that it would be too much for her and she might hurt herself. Brianne insisted on going because she knew she could handle it. She pleaded and finally her parents and doctors gave in.

Brianne found a local bank that helped collect the supplies. Then she got people to sort the supplies and help her take them to Iowa. Brianne was on the news because everyone was surprised that a person with OI would risk her health to help others. Brianne made a big splash in Iowa. Not only had she brought much-needed supplies, but she also brought a wonderful sense of humor and a great smile. Because of her efforts to help during the flood, Brianne received the National Caring Award. It has been given to other

Schwantes family

*Brianne has met First Lady Hilary Clinton and other leaders.*

special people like Jimmy Carter and Jane Goodall. While she was in Iowa, she met Tony Rodham, First Lady Hilary Clinton's brother. Rodham told President Clinton about Brianne, and a few months later she was invited to the White House to meet the president and vice president. President Clinton was so impressed with Brianne that he invited her to Denver, Colorado, during the pope's visit for World Youth Day.

Brianne and her sister were both blessed by Pope John Paul II, and it was a really exciting time. People from all over the country were in Denver to see the pope, so every place the pope went was crowded. Brianne and her family were at the airport for his arrival. The Secret Service ushered her family straight up front so President Clinton could find them. Brianne said there must have been more than a thousand people there. They were all trying to get up front, so some kids from the World Youth Organization helped protect the family from getting crunched. When the pope arrived, President Clinton had him go straight to Brianne to meet her. It was very exciting.

Brianne has another interesting story about meeting a president. President Bush was going to talk about Brianne in a speech, so he invited her to a ribbon cutting ceremony at the Children's Inn in Washington, D.C. The ceremony was outside and Brianne got really hot. She wasn't supposed to go inside the Children's Inn, but because she was so small she just snuck right past the guards and Secret Service agents. She sat down on a bench. Then a lady came and sat down next to her. After

talking with her for a while, Brianne realized that she had been talking to the president's wife, Barbara Bush. Brianne said Mrs. Bush was a very nice lady.

Brianne's family is pretty normal. Her family has a total of four people. One thing, though, is really unusual. Her mom's name is Terry and so is her dad's! Her sister's name is Elizabeth, but they call her Lizzy for short. Her parents try not to make a big deal out of Brianne's OI, but they can't help worrying. They also worry that Lizzy won't get as much attention as Brianne, so they work extra hard to have a close family and give everyone a lot of love.

Brianne's family enjoys doing things together. They build models and are building a dollhouse. On cold days, they love to play board games. They have a pool in their backyard. They swim a lot to keep Brianne's bones strong. The family enjoys their cats and sometimes spoils them. Their cats names are Stitches and Chica. Chica has a spine problem. This makes it hard for her to use her back legs very well. They found Chica at someone's house where there was a sign out for free kittens. Chica was a little kitten who was hiding in a dirty part of the garage. When they lifted her up, they saw that her legs were twisted and turned. Brianne asked about this and was told that a couple of the kittens had been born this way. Having a kitten who has to work harder to do normal things has made Brianne appreciate her parents more. She understands how exciting it is to see someone you love be successful at something that seemed impossible for them to do.

Brianne's family likes to take trips. One time Brianne was awarded a trip to Disney World through the Make-A-Wish Foundation. Some of the people working at school sent Brianne's name in to the organization that gives these trips, and the group picked her name. The whole family got to go. Brianne could not go on many of the rides, but she did go on the Lazy River and other water rides. That didn't stop the family from having fun. Lizzy went on all the roller coaster rides, and they had a great time just being together.

Brianne has many hobbies. Since she has to be careful when she is outside, especially in bad weather, she does a lot of inside things. Brianne works on many crafts. She is working on a quilt with her mom, and she can't wait to snuggle up

inside it. She also does cross-stitch. She invites her friends over to make cookies and they try really hard not to burn any. She enjoys collecting penguins and has lots of them in all shapes and sizes. They are made from many different materials, including glass and china, and some are stuffed animals.

Brianne enjoys school. She loves languages so she is taking a lot of foreign language courses. When she gets older, she'd like to work in international relations. She is also involved in debate and forensics. These are extracurricular activities in which students compete with other schools. Debate is where you take an issue and argue for one side or the other. Forensics is where kids give a dramatic or humorous reading. Both of these activities will help Brianne in the future with her career. What Brianne would really like to do is work for the United Nations. We think Brianne would be great at this. After all, she has already given many speeches to the government.

Brianne's heroes are people like President Clinton. She likes him because she feels he's a great leader. She also thinks of pilot Amelia Earhart as a hero because she was very dedicated to what she was doing. She was willing to go out and do something that others were afraid to do. Amelia Earhart was courageous and flew out into the world even though she didn't know what was ahead of her.

Brianne is a very courageous girl who has helped people through rough times. Even though Brianne has a disease, it doesn't keep her from helping people in need. She helps people even if it means

risking her health. She also believes in never giving up, and it is a lifelong goal of hers to make other people's lives better.

## Here is a letter from Brianne:

*Remember to treat others the way you want to be treated! You don't have to be super strong to make a difference in someone's life. I want to give my strengths to others to help them. Because of OI, I needed a lot of help from others as a child. It is important to give back to the people around you, but volunteering isn't just giving back what people gave you. I hope you will volunteer because it will make you feel great. When you see how much you add to another person's life, you will understand how important your help has been. Just take the time to get involved and be there for those who might need you.*

*My best advice to you is to believe in yourself. When you do this you can achieve your goals. I believed in myself and, because of this, others learned to believe in me as well. You can do what you set your mind to do if you just believe!*

*Thanks again for reading my story.*

# MELISSA POE
*Environmental Activist*

Melissa Poe might be young now, but she hopes to live until she's 100 years old. She also knows she might not get the chance to live tomorrow if the problems with our environment don't change today. This thought helped Melissa decide at a young age that she had to do something to help the world now. She knew that if she was going to make it to her one hundredth birthday, she would need to start making a difference before her tenth.

It all started when Melissa saw a TV commercial that said kids were dying from pollution. She asked her mother if she was going to die from pollution. Melissa was shocked when her mother answered,

"Maybe." Even though Melissa was young, she decided she needed to do something about it. Melissa felt so strongly about her right to survive that she thought President George Bush should know about it, too. That's why she wrote him a letter. She wrote:

*Dear Mr. President,*

*Please will you do something about pollution? I want to live till I am 100 years old.*

*Mr. President, if you ignore this letter, we will all die of pollution and the ozone layer.*

*Please help,*

*Melissa Poe, age 9*

Poe family

*Melissa took her message to the president and beyond.*

When President Bush did not respond, she got a billboard company in Washington, D.C., to print part of her letter on a large billboard closer to the president's house. But she still waited for his reply. She kept herself busy by working with her environmental club.

In the fall of 1989, Melissa started an environmental club for kids called Kids FACE. It stands for Kids for a Clean Environment. The members started working for a better environment by doing things like local cleanups, letter-writing campaigns, saying no to Styrofoam and lots of packaging on new items, planting trees, conserving energy and water, and recycling. They really started making a difference even in their own neighborhood.

When Melissa finally heard from the president, she was sad and disappointed because he didn't want to change anything. She felt that he still hadn't heard her message, but she has kept trying to help the environment anyway. She got herself on a morning news show, NBC's *Today*, to talk about problems with the environment. She was also interviewed by other news shows, radio stations, newspapers, and magazines. Pretty soon, more billboards had Melissa's message on them. All together, more than 250 billboards have carried Melissa's message.

As more kids learned about Melissa's club, they wrote letters to join. Melissa did not ignore their letters because she knows how awful that feels. Instead, Kids FACE sent them membership books, certificates, and lots of free information about how to start new chapters at their own schools. Membership is free, and the club grew and grew.

Now Kids FACE has more than 300,000 members. There are more than 300 chapters across the United States and even more chapters in foreign countries. It is an international organization that has programs to get kids involved in helping the earth. It also has a newsletter that gives all the members lots of interesting information about problems with animals and the environment. It even tells kids what kinds of things they can do to help solve some of these tough problems.

If you want to join Kids FACE, you

can find more information in the resource section of this book. The headquarters is in Nashville, Tennessee, where Melissa and her family live. She lives with her mother, Trish, and her father, Pat. Her brother, Mason, is older and he lives on his own.

We think Melissa is a hero because she is getting other kids involved, and because she hasn't given up on helping the environment. She knows just how to get the job done and she says, "If you see a problem in the world, you need to get involved and not wait around for others to solve it. You should do it yourself."

# CHARLIE WOLFE
## *Poet Helps Stop Violence*

The world needs more people like Charlie Wolfe. He has gone through some very heartbreaking things throughout his 20 years. And yet, somehow, through it all, he's kept very calm and cool. He's found a way to express his emotions and feelings so that they don't hurt anyone.

When Charlie was born, his parents were older than usual. He had one sister and three brothers. They were all more than 12 years older than him. Charlie's oldest brother, Chris, was 18 when Charlie was born. Charlie's sister was also much older and almost like another mother to him. In fact, when she got married and moved away from home, Charlie said he felt like she had divorced him.

Charlie's dad worked at a classical music station for over 30 years. When Charlie used to get bored, he would turn on the radio and listen to his dad. His mom is a very spunky lady and she has lots of energy. She stayed home to take care of Charlie when he was young. Later, she went to work as a nurse's aide.

Charlie's older brothers and sister used to drag him a lot of places. He got to go to high school ball games and do many different things with them. One time, when one of them took him to the high school, he had to sit in the principal's office to wait for his sister while she was in class. Sometimes some of them would buy him a pop and Ding-Dongs and tell him not to tell Mom and Dad. The first thing Charlie did when he got home was tell his folks about it.

*Charlie talks to the Westridge authors.*

Charlie told us that he sometimes bothered his older brothers and they would get mad. Charlie laughs about it when he remembers the time they tied him up and put a stack of lawn chairs on top of him. His mother had to come and rescue him.

Charlie's family did lots of different things together. Every year the whole bunch would go to see the *Nutcracker* because his dad got tickets from the radio station where he worked. The family also had an old baby blue Volkswagen Bug that Charlie liked a lot. They would all squeeze into the car and go for a trip in the mountains. One time they went on a four-wheel-drive road and got stuck. They all had to get out and push. Charlie was so little he got carried down the trail.

When Charlie was in first grade, he went to a private school. He had lots and lots of homework every night. Through the years in private school, he struggled with his reading and writing. Later, when Charlie's dad lost his job in the radio business, Charlie had to go back to public schools. He didn't like it because he got letters from other boys threatening to beat him up. He soon learned he had to gain the respect of the other boys. Some of the boys got to be his friends later.

Charlie went to a neighborhood high school. It was rough and he had very few friends. The friends he had wanted to be violent and do bad things. When Charlie's friend Josh was about 17 years old, he got involved with a gang. Josh told Charlie some of the bad things he had done, like drive-by shootings. Josh kept on asking Charlie to join the gang. Charlie knew he didn't belong in a gang and that gangs were wrong and they wouldn't get him anywhere except arrested or killed. He turned Josh down. Charlie warned Josh that he would end up in prison or dead. And that is what happened. Josh was shot by a member of a different gang. When this happened, Charlie had so many emotions at one time that he didn't know what to do. Charlie was terrified.

Josh was not Charlie's only friend with a problem. Another friend started drinking when he was young. He had a bad drinking problem and he couldn't stop. A doctor tried to help, but it was too late. Charlie went to the hospital to see his friend when he was in a coma. Soon he died. Charlie still remembers how his friend looked in the coffin—like someone had drained the life out of him. He was gone and Charlie couldn't talk to him anymore. He could only pray for him. Charlie knew it would be hard, but he had to go on.

Another friend of Charlie's was caught selling drugs to an undercover cop. He was arrested and put in jail. Charlie remembers going to visit Jason. When he walked into the jail it looked just like the movies. He had to sit on a hard metal stool, talk on a telephone, and look through bulletproof glass. Charlie said he saw something in Jason's eyes that he had never seen before. It was a different look, sort of cold, lost, and confused. This was a wake-up call for Charlie. It told him he should never do what Jason had done.

These things have encouraged Charlie to stay out of gangs and not use drugs and alcohol. Charlie knew he had to change some things. His friends were a bad influence and the structure of his high school wasn't right for him. He was having trouble in math and English. He did not think he fit in. He never really said much in class and he just felt out of place. Every morning Charlie would try to think of an excuse so he could stay home. That's when he started looking for another school.

After searching, Charlie decided to go to an alternative high school, and he loved it. The best thing about this school was that people were not allowed to fight or they would get kicked out. For most people, it was their last chance to get an education.

At the alternative school, Charlie liked the special activities. One time his class went on a trip to the Navajo reservation in northeastern Arizona. Charlie's class decided they wanted to replace the fruit trees Kit Carson had burned on the reservation in 1859, so the group planted new trees in two canyons there.

The trip was very important to Charlie because he learned many things about the Navajos and himself. Charlie enjoyed the silence on the reservation. At times it seemed so quiet you could hear a pin drop. One of the elders shared a lesson with him about the two-to-one ratio. The elder said that you have two eyes, two ears, and one mouth. Therefore, you should look and listen twice as much as you speak. This made Charlie feel very good because he had always enjoyed sitting and watching quietly.

Beside the neat activities, the high school had fun classes. One of Charlie's favorite classes was his poetry class. He liked to listen to the sound of the words. His teacher said he had the eye of a poet because he could see a different side of things. Positive changes started to happen for Charlie at this school. He felt better and started sharing his thoughts and ideas in his classes. He learned he did have something to share.

His favorite person at the school was a teacher named Richard who encouraged him to graduate. At this school, all the students called the teachers by their first names. Charlie thought of Richard as a second dad. They are still good friends today.

One day when Charlie was a senior in high school, he was chosen to take his favorite poet, Jimmy Baca, around town. He couldn't believe his ears! He was going to give a tour to Jimmy Baca! That night

Charlie was so nervous he didn't sleep. All he could do was think about his hero.

Jimmy Baca was a professional poet from New Mexico. Long ago Jimmy went to prison. He learned his lesson the hard way. He had a lot of time to think about his life and what he wanted to do with it. When he got out of jail, Jimmy started an organization to promote the arts by expressing anger in artistic ways. He also became a poet and wrote a book.

When Charlie took Jimmy Baca on the tour, Charlie was still nervous, but he lived through it. Charlie treated Jimmy like a regular person, not like a famous superstar. That's why they became good friends. Jimmy gave him some really good advice about his life. He told Charlie, "You are afraid and angry. You shouldn't let it out in violence but in an artistic way like poetry." He explained how Charlie shouldn't show anger by fighting. Jimmy helped Charlie make some good decisions in life.

Charlie took Jimmy's advice and he became more serious about writing poetry. Charlie writes about his life. He enjoys words and he has a very good vocabulary. His spelling isn't always perfect, but he doesn't let it stand in his way. He expresses his feelings in his poems. Some of the poems he keeps to himself, and some of them he shares. Whenever Charlie is frustrated or feeling low, he pulls out a pencil and paper and starts to write poetry about what he feels. He advises other people to do the same.

We heard a few of his poems, and we had strong feelings about them. Charlie taught us that poetry is more than rhyming words. It can be anything you want. He encouraged us to write poetry, too.

When Charlie is writing his poems at home, sometimes he gets frustrated. If he is so angry he can't work, he does sit-ups, push-ups, and deep breathing exercises. This helps him get rid of his frustrations. He knows this is a good way to handle negative thoughts. When he has calmed himself down, he writes poetry. Sometimes Charlie digs deep into his mind, and it hurts a lot. At times he stays up late and writes for several hours to finish his poems.

When Charlie was feeling bad about his friend who was shot, he wrote this poem:

### Life Short Friend

*It was over a year since*
*I'd talked to him*
*but we were friends*

*We would go to parties*
*on the weekends*
*in my big old truck*

*We always had women around*
*like mosquitoes in the summer*
*Like everything else*
*he wanted them all*
*all from everyone*
*and at the same time*
*giving nothing*
*but promises as empty*
*as his future*

*My friend sought*
*the easy way out*

*like a lab rat in a maze*
*I remember someone was*
*forever having to watch his back*
*like a big brother in*
*grade school*

*I also remember*
*reading the newspaper*
*article with its*
*headline*
*"One Teen Wounded, Another Killed"*
*It was outside a North side Circle K*
*that my friend was just another*
*teen killed*

*It was in his girlfriend's Bronco*
*which he bled*
*on the way to the hospital*
*he spoke his last words*
*"I'm cool now, I'm cool."*

*He was cool*
*and stiff*
*on the slab at the*
*morgue*

When Charlie is done writing a poem, he takes time to think. He reads it over and says to himself, "Wow, this is why I was upset. Now it all makes sense." Sometimes, Charlie goes to places where someone is singing the blues. There, he drinks a strong coffee and lets his feelings flow out of him in poetry. Sometimes he reads poems to other people.

Charlie met a woman who helped kids in trouble by using poetry. She asked him if he would like to help her with some of the kids at a detention center called the Lost and Found. Charlie was anxious to help the kids. The night before he was going to the center, Charlie was worried and he could not go to sleep. The next day, as Charlie drove up the winding canyon road, he wondered how the kids ended up in the center. He wondered if something bad would happen when he talked to them.

Charlie took a deep breath and stepped into the old, run-down center. He saw holes in the walls and old secondhand furniture. The kids that had been placed at the center had lots of problems. They didn't know how to express their anger and emotions in a positive way. Charlie was so nervous that he had sweaty palms and a bad taste in his mouth. When he first saw the group of boys, he thought it was going to be rough. Their expressions and gang symbols didn't help to ease his feelings. Charlie remembers one kid in particular who scared him half to death. He had tattoos up and down his arms.

As Charlie sat there waiting for his turn to speak, an older poet talked. The 17 young men didn't seem interested. They acted bored and squirmed in their seats. Charlie kept wondering if he too would bore them. He had butterflies in his stomach. When he finally started to talk, he felt half of them weren't listening to him. He was afraid they wouldn't like his poetry. Then he told them about his hero, Jimmy Baca.

When Charlie started to read his poems, the kids knew he had some of the same feelings they had experienced. When Charlie looked up, he realized the kids were listening and responding. When he was

done, the boys stood up and clapped. This made Charlie feel great. He said to himself, "This is not so bad after all."

When Charlie went back to the center, he felt more comfortable with the kids. He worked with the young men for many months. Charlie got them started writing poems. They learned that a poem was a lot more than a greeting card. They began expressing their emotions through poetry. He helped the kids find out who they really were. They depended on Charlie because he was close to their age and he understood them. The teens started improving the way in which they expressed anger. All of them started reading and writing poems. Charlie felt sad when he could no longer work with the kids at the Lost and Found, but he knew he had helped them and that made him feel good inside.

Charlie has also given presentations in schools. He usually wears T-shirts designed by Black Mesa Enterprises. Sometimes they have a design on them done by an ex–gang member. Charlie shares stories about his friends who died to show that violence isn't the answer. He tells how he learned to get the anger out of himself by writing. He reads poetry and helps kids think about using artistic ways to express their emotions.

In 1995 Charlie moved to Albuquerque, New Mexico. Charlie went there to work with his friend, Jimmy Baca. For Charlie, this was a dream come true. Today, Charlie and Jimmy are still helping young people through poetry. They have run some literacy programs in which they try to teach others the love of knowledge and books instead of violence.

Charlie is helping high school kids and telling them to stay off drugs and out of gangs. He still remembers Jimmy's advice and he is still passing it along to others. Charlie's dreams are coming true because he is helping young people learn a nonviolent way of life.

Charlie Wolfe has done something heroic. He didn't save someone's life or catch an evil villain, but he is making a difference helping others. And no, Charlie isn't Superman. But he is a role model to us. Many kids have the wrong heroes, but surely we don't, because Charlie Wolfe is our hero.

## Here is a letter from Charlie:

*I have found a peace in myself by thinking about what's important to me. Spend a lot of time with yourself and get to know who you are. You are the most important person in your life. You need to grow and learn from all the things around you. Look at your dreams and desires and set your goals. I have found that*

*Charlie is a role model for younger kids.*

Westridge Young Writers Workshop

*sharing my life experiences helped me grow into a better person. I have a rule that I will always value the beauty of the earth and God's gifts to me through the people He puts into my life.*

*Don't let people talk you into doing things you don't want to do. It's your life and you have to live it. If someone tells you to do things you don't like, follow your heart. Your friend isn't a friend if he is willing to get you hurt. He may not be with you in ten years. Only you will be with yourself.*

*I search for truth and try to share it with those around me. Learn from the world around you. I hope that you will never end your search for truth and that you will find out who you need to be.*

### *A Poem*

*The world of poetry*
*fits loose like my pants*
*do*
*no confining punctuation*
*and no use for*
*grammar anyway*
*words are*
*grease splattered on*
*paper walls*

**Here are a few more of Charlie's poems:**

### *The Ladder*

*Through the passage of time*
*And the accumulation of history*
*I've made my foundation*

*In the absence of time*
*but with a high regard for history*
*I've made this window*
*of my dreams*

*But to get there*
*I've got to build the ladder*

# KORY JOHNSON
*Friend of the Earth*

In the small minority neighborhood of Maryvale, Arizona, another person died. In 1989, Amy Johnson died of heart disease at the age of 16. Her heart problems were caused by the contaminated well water her mom drank while she was pregnant.

Amy's sister, Kory Johnson, was just 11 years old when Amy died. Then Kory's mother, Terri, got cancer and had to undergo major surgery. Kory's grandmother also died of cancer at the age of 55. Within just a few years, there were 31 cancer deaths in the small community. The residents knew it was a problem with their environment. So, at a young age, Kory Johnson became determined to stop the poisoning of the earth.

Kory started giving up all her free time to help the earth. Kory is president of Children for a Safe Environment (CSE). She started this group in 1988 with four of her friends. Her group now has more than 300 members from many states. CSE started taking on battles over environmental problems that harm kids. Kory has talked to politicians and important officials in organizations like the EPA (Environmental Protection Agency).

After an incinerator was built in a poor Arizona neighborhood, Children for a Safe Environment fought against it. Working with groups like Greenpeace, Kory and her group fought against the incinerator for two years. They talked to their City Council, protested, and wrote letters. They held a candlelight vigil, and they had a display

Johnson family

*Kory took a stand against pollution.*

so they will be aware of what people are doing to our environment. She hopes they won't make the same mistakes in the future. That way, when they have children, their environment will be clean and healthy.

Kory and CSE have worked hard to try to stop the destruction of our world. They've distributed canvas shopping bags, organized neighborhood cleanups, and done a lot of recycling. They've stopped two toxic dumps from being built. CSE wrote letters to the owner of McDonald's asking them to stop using Styrofoam containers. They agreed, so they don't use the containers anymore. Kory even got an award from the mayor for getting the city to stop using Styrofoam.

Kory has won many other awards for her efforts to help the environment. She was the first to receive the Windstar Youth Award. Another award given to her was the People Who Care Award from Channel 12 in Arizona. They gave her $1,000 with this award, and Kory gave half of the money to charity.

Kory also likes to help out other people. She has volunteered to help at the local Ronald McDonald House. Kory and her mother raised money to rent a camp to give a vacation to 40 campers who have AIDS. Kory lives with her mother in Phoenix, Arizona. They like to work together to solve problems.

Kory has taken some big risks while she fights for a safe environment. Once she was arrested for standing in front of a dump truck. The truck was full of dirt containing DDT, a dangerous pesticide. She was trying to stop it from contaminating the landfill

of kids environmental artwork. Other kids listened and joined Kory's group. Pretty soon the adults were listening to the kids. Greenpeace set up an office in Kory's house. Finally, the incinerator was shut down before it started burning any hazardous waste.

Kory has traveled to many places to speak to other kids about solving problems with the environment. In Arizona, she has gone to schools to talk to kids about recycling and the environment. She tells them about environmental racism, which is when a business or the government takes advantage of poor communities by polluting their neighborhoods or giving them hazardous jobs. Kory speaks to other kids near a grade school. Instead of getting a medal for her efforts, she was fined 16 hours of community service. This was okay with Kory because she likes to help with her community and the environment anyway. She says she always prefers to solve problems the legal way, but sometimes waiting for the officials can create even bigger problems to solve later.

Today Kory is continuing her work by fighting for environmental rights. You can join Kory's club no matter where you live. Look for the address in the Arizona section of the Resource Guide (page 103). Kory hopes Children for a Safe Environment will always work for positive changes.

### Kory says:

*A lot of people are afraid to fight because they trust their city officials to always do what's right. That needs to change. No matter what happens, you always have to stick up for what you believe in. We have to stop bad things from happening to kids. Keep fighting, and don't give up for anything.*

# DAVID LEVITT
## *Helping Feed the Hungry*

The next time you are reading the newspaper and laughing at the comics, remember there are other things in the paper that might also entertain you. Sometimes an article in the paper can lead you in the right direction. Here's the story of a young man who read about an interesting organization in the Sunday paper. The organization ended up changing his life and many of the lives around him.

David Levitt lives in Seminole, Florida. In many ways he's just an average everyday kid who likes to play basketball, volleyball, and wrestle. David's best friend's name is Adam, and the boys play in a band and go to school together. David plays the piano and Adam plays the drums. David loves '50s and '60s rock 'n' roll. He sings and plays in a group called Celebration. He loves computers, playing Sega, reading R. L. Stine mysteries, and watching TV. David has taken part in children's theater since he was eight years old. He has learned to speak in front of large groups. He likes school and finds it pretty easy. His hardest course is advanced science, but it is also his favorite course. When he grows up, he wants to be a lawyer, a broadcast journalist, or attend the Air Force Academy and become an officer in the United States Air Force.

David lives with his mom, dad, and older sister Jamie. His dad, Richard, is part owner of a company that sells medical equipment. His mom, Sandy, works as a bookkeeper three days a week and does volunteer work. David's parents have taught

Levitt family

*David had a dream of helping others.*

him to be proud of his Jewish heritage. They have encouraged him to try to pass on his beliefs and traditions to future generations. His family believes that being a good Jew means not only going to services regularly, but also doing good deeds in the community.

David began studying for his bar mitzvah, a celebration in his Jewish faith. According to Jewish tradition, a bar mitzvah celebration is for a young boy when he becomes a responsible man. It is a time to celebrate becoming 13 years old. Before his bar mitzvah, a boy must learn Hebrew, be able to read many Jewish prayers, and learn to read from the Torah, the holiest Jewish book. David's parents told him that not only would he be learning some very important Jewish customs, but it would also be a time to do a special good deed. This good deed was meant to help the community and help David learn about being a responsible citizen. David thought this sounded like an interesting thing so he

began looking for something he could do to help others.

In March 1993, David was reading the *Parade Magazine* from the newspaper. It had an article about Stan Curtis, the man who had set up Kentucky Harvest. It told how Kentucky Harvest takes leftover food from restaurants and gives it to the homeless. Mr. Curtis started this group when he learned that many of the restaurants in his neighborhood were throwing away good food because it didn't look nice enough to serve to customers. He decided that there must be a way to put this food to good use. So Mr. Curtis asked volunteers to pick up this unused food and deliver it to shelters for the needy. David thought this was a neat idea.

Since Mr. Curtis' program was in Kentucky and David lived in Florida, David needed to see if there was an organization like Kentucky Harvest near him. David and his mom found Tampa Bay Harvest. It was an organization close to David and a lot like Mr. Curtis' organization. David went to a meeting for the organization and talked to the president, Mary

Levitt family

*When David turned 13, he was bar mitzvahed.*

Dowdell. He wanted to know what things he could do to help out. Mary told him about a program that had been used in the Louisville school district in Kentucky. The leftover food from the school cafeterias was packaged and sent to shelters for people who needed help.

David went home that night and talked to his parents about the school program. They thought it was a great idea, so David decided to ask his principal if the leftover cafeteria food from his school could be donated to Tampa Bay Harvest. He didn't even hesitate. The very next day he went right to school to talk to his principal. His principal said it sounded like a good idea, but it would probably be too much of a hassle. David didn't think it would be that hard, but his plan was turned down.

David was very disappointed, but he and his family talked again about the plan. His family encouraged him not to give up. They told him that if he really believed in something he should stand up for it. They decided that maybe David needed to go to the school board to see about his plan. David wrote a letter describing the plan and Tampa Bay Harvest. He also included information in the letter about Florida's Good

Samaritan law. This law says that anyone who gives food to the hungry can't get into trouble if someone should get sick. He sent a letter to the superintendent of schools and to every member of the School Board.

After the superintendent read the letter, David called and talked with him about his ideas. He felt his personal phone call would show the School Board how serious he was. David talked to all the School Board members, and they all seemed interested. They set up a meeting with David to talk more about it. The meeting was on November 10, 1993, David's twelfth birthday. He felt like his greatest birthday gift would be the School Board okaying his idea. He was nervous, but he told them about Tampa Bay Harvest and his plans. The School Board unanimously agreed to the plan. They set up a special meeting between the Tampa Bay Harvest director and the school system's Food Services director to work out the details. They needed to make a plan to package the food in the right kind of containers and get everything picked up and delivered. David was told that it would take a few months to get the plan going.

During all this time, David continued working with the Tampa Bay Harvest, delivering food and going to many different shelters. He was learning about how the shelters worked and who the shelters helped. He realized all homeless people were not the same. A lot of them were like the people in his neighborhood. He knew he wanted to do more. Halloween was coming up and David decided to trick-or-treat for canned food. He went out and collected about 60 pounds of food in 45 minutes.

David's actions were making the news, and articles were written about him in the newspaper. Because of his efforts, he received the Citizen of the Month Award from Saturn Automobiles of Clearwater. His middle school also awarded him with a Student of the Month plaque. Pretty neat for a 12 year old!

While David was waiting for the School Board to finish their plans, he went to a mall near his home. It was almost Christmas and the need for food was greater. At the mall, David spoke to the restaurant managers about what they could do to help. He told them about Tampa Bay Harvest and the procedures it used. Several of the managers were interested. They made plans to learn more about the program and to get involved.

This was an important time for David because he was spending more and more time learning and speaking about the Tampa Bay Harvest. He was really learning his stuff. He knew all the procedures by heart. He learned more from this project than he ever expected. David learned how

*David meets with Kentucky Harvest founder Stan Curtis and Tampa Bay Harvest president Mary Dowdell.*

Levitt family

*David picks up a bread donation for Tampa Bay Harvest.*

different people lived in his community and how to get others interested in helping.

In April, Tampa Bay Harvest held its first Plant the Seed dinner. This event was meant to publicize the group's efforts and get more people involved with helping. David was invited to speak at the dinner. It was a wonderful night for David. He couldn't believe his good luck. He got to meet Stan Curtis, the man who started it all. What a thrill! He also met Miss America, Kim Aiken. Wow!

David was really anxious to get things going with the schools, and it seemed like the project was taking forever. After a few months had gone by, David checked to find out how the School Board was doing with his plan. He learned that the Health

Department was insisting on airtight containers to deliver the food. The School Board did not have money for the containers. This new problem could have meant an end to all his work because, without these containers, Tampa Bay Harvest couldn't deliver the food. David knew he had gone too far to stop. He came up with another idea. He wrote to Rubbermaid, Ziploc, and other companies that manufacture containers to store food. He did a good job telling them about his plan and its problems. The companies were so impressed with David's efforts that they sent eight cases of Gladlock storage bags and a gift certificate to buy storage containers. David was thrilled because now the plan was back in action.

In August David learned that the plans were almost finished and it wouldn't be long before the program was started. He was excited because it had been a long year of hard work. In October 1994, David went to a School Board meeting to see his finished plans. Two weeks later his dreams became real and ten schools started the project. They had expected to get about 100 pounds of food a week, but instead they received well over 300 pounds. Pretty soon more schools were added. The goal was to have the entire school system, all 92 schools, donating food. David couldn't believe it. All of his work had paid off.

At the end of November, David was bar mitzvahed. It had been a busy year working on the food plan and studying Hebrew and Jewish traditions. He felt he had learned how to serve his community, and he was ready to accept the responsibilities of being an adult in his religion. He asked everyone who was invited to his bar mitzvah service to bring cans of food to donate. During his service, David shared what he had learned. He said that he knew he could help others but he didn't know just how good helping others would make him feel. He knew it was all worth it. That afternoon at his party, his friends and family brought in a total of 500 pounds of canned food. It was a terrific end to his day, but not an end to his volunteer work helping others or the effects of his plan.

During the 1994–1995 school year, 55,000 pounds of food were donated to Tampa Bay Harvest because of David's plan. During the 1995–1996 school year, all the schools in the district participated and donated a total of 134,000 pounds of food. David is now working with his state representative to get his plan passed statewide so that all the Florida schools can donate their food.

Because of his hard work and dedication, David was awarded the Prudential Spirit of Community Award. He was also featured on *Nick News*. In the spring of 1996, First Lady Hillary Clinton gave David a very special award. It was a Point of Light, an award given by the president to people who have made a real difference. On July 3, 1996, David was chosen to run with the Olympic torch in St. Petersburg, Florida. The eternal Olympic flame is the symbol of the Olympic Games. It traveled all the way from Greece to Georgia for the 1996 Summer Games. What a special honor that must have been!

## Here is a message from David:

*Don't let anyone tell you that you are too young to do things. Anyone can make a difference if they'll just try! Just because you're a kid doesn't mean you can't make something good happen. Get involved. Kids can do as much as adults. Pick a project you're interested in and do some research on it. Go to where they meet and talk to the leaders. If you're still interested in it, volunteer to help. After you get involved, stick with it. Things don't always happen overnight. Keep going. Remember, all your efforts will be worth it.*

# CHRISTY SURRENCY
## *Showing a Positive Attitude*

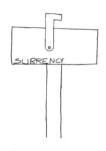

One late afternoon Christy's dad was driving home. He came to a sudden stop. There, on the side of the road, he saw a very tiny kitten. He pulled over and got the kitten out of the dirt. He felt sorry for the little kitten, and he took it home to his house so that Christy could take care of it.

After a short time, Christy's family found out that something was wrong with the cat. They'd call for the cat they had named Shelby, but she wouldn't come. Christy had her mother hold Shelby, then Christy stood behind them and screamed. Shelby didn't react, so they decided that she was deaf. They learned to get Shelby's attention by waving their arms around and flashing the lights on and off.

Shelby and Christy have a special bond. It seemed amazing that Shelby ended up at Christy's house, especially since they have something so unique in common. Both Christy and her kitten have a hearing loss.

Christy was born on November 18, 1974. Her parents are Eddie and Sandra Surrency. Christy grew up in the small town of Odum, Georgia. She is an only child. Christy comes from a Christian family that has a strong faith in God. They live out in the country, right down the road from her grandparents. Her grandparents own a small farm, and Christy has spent a lot of time with them. Both of Christy's parents work at a

*Beauty queen Christy*

local pulp mill that makes chemical cellulose, a product that goes into things such as camera film, filters, baby diapers, tires, and much more.

Christy's father owns horses. He likes to collect old horse buggies. Christy and her dad like to take the buggies out on holidays. Christy is also very close to her mother and they are each other's best friends.

Christy was 18 months old when she had her first surgery to put tubes in her ears. When her hearing did not improve, she had tubes put in three more times over the years. Christy felt discouraged. The doctors thought her hearing would be better, but it wasn't. When Christy entered school, her parents felt that they had to let Christy be on her own. Although they loved her very much,

they knew that they couldn't hold Christy down. She had a very independent spirit, and they believed she should have the chance to try for everything she wanted in her life, even with a hearing loss.

Christy did not know that she was losing more hearing. It all happened so slowly. When Christy began to realize that her hearing was getting worse, she did not want to tell her parents that she was not hearing well. Her parents did not have a clue what was happening. School got harder for Christy. She couldn't hear her teacher very well so she learned to read lips. Her hearing got worse and worse. Whenever the teacher turned around, Christy couldn't see her lips. She didn't know what the teacher was saying, and she couldn't understand what was happening.

Fourth grade, with the added homework and harder assignments, was really difficult for Christy. She had to take more responsibility and pay attention more carefully. Her parents started to wonder about her hearing when Christy wouldn't come when she was called or did not hear the phone ring unless it was in the same room with her. Christy still tried to keep her secret. She did not want to get hearing aids because she didn't want to look funny. She wanted to be like the other kids. She didn't want to be teased for being different.

Christy was very excited to get out of elementary school and go on to junior high. She had grown up in a small town with a population of 382 and she knew everyone. She was anxious to meet new people. Christy thought junior high would be exciting because she would get to meet kids from other towns. At the same time, Christy also felt nervous and afraid that she might be teased by other kids. She rode the bus from Odum, her hometown, to Jesup, where she went to school. Her school was made up of kids from three towns (Jesup, Odum, and Screven) because the towns were too small to have their own junior high or high schools.

Finally, when she was 13 years old, Christy realized she couldn't go on keeping her secret about her hearing. She talked to her parents and decided to get hearing aids. It was a tough challenge, but it made Christy stronger. She learned to believe in herself, and that's when things started to change.

Christy blossomed in junior high.

She started to take dance lessons. When people don't have all their hearing they usually don't have good balance, but Christy was determined to learn how to dance. She had to work hard. With lots of practice she began to dance very well and started feeling more confident about herself. Christy had a strong desire to help other people, and teaching dance was something she felt she could share.

In high school, Christy started volunteering at a local center for people with disabilities. One of her volunteer jobs was to help the people who were handicapped learn to dance. Christy said it was always fun to see the smiles on their faces. She told us that helping these people helped her more than she could ever have helped them. They taught her to love the simple things in life and to always be a loyal friend.

*Christy and a young friend ride in an old-fashioned horse and buggy.*

Surrency family

Christy also worked with people who competed in the Special Olympics. She helped one woman who was handicapped. Christy said she'll never forget the look on the woman's face when she crossed the finish line in first place.

When Christy was doing volunteer work for one of her classes, she met Marci. Marci was a 13-year-old girl who attended a local Wayne County school and later attended Georgia School for the Deaf. When Christy first met her, Marci seemed sad, lonely, and unhappy with her life. Christy could see that Marci had low self-esteem. Christy kept watching Marci and wanted to get to know her better, but they couldn't find the time. Christy finally called Marci's mom and explained that she also had a hearing problem and

would like to meet with Marci and try to help her. Christy and Marci started to work together and got to know each other. Soon they started to giggle and joke around and they developed a good friendship.

As Christy got to know Marci better, she talked Marci into entering some beauty pageants. Marci even ran for homecoming queen at her school. One girl ran from each class, and all the kids in the school voted for the winner. At the homecoming football game, Marci was crowned queen. She thanked Christy for helping her learn to believe in herself.

Marci and Christy are still friends. Marci uses sign language and is teaching Christy to sign, too. Even though Christy is away at college, the girls still keep in touch with each other.

When Christy was a senior in high school she heard about a man named Max Cleland who was Georgia's secretary of state. Christy was impressed with him because he was a disabled Vietnam veteran who had done so much with his life. He lost his legs in the war, and he was in a wheelchair. Secretary of State Cleland became Christy's personal hero. When Christy met him, she told him that she wanted to do more for people with disabilities. He appointed Christy to be on the governor's Committee on Employment of People with Disabilities.

Christy traveled to Atlanta, Georgia, the state capital, for the meetings. The committee met in a big fancy room. Christy sat in a large leather chair and felt very important. She was one of the

SUPER Bowl 29

youngest people on the committee. At first she was nervous, but soon the other members saw that Christy could help them. Because she had a disability, she could be their expert.

Christy was chosen by the committee to help volunteers learn to work with people with handicaps for the Annual Convention on Disabilities. She trained 50 volunteers to become guides for the people with disabilities who were coming to the convention. In her meetings, Christy would tell the volunteers the do's and don'ts for helping people. For example, she told them it is always a good thing to offer your help, but not to help without asking. In addition, you should make eye contact with people and speak to them directly as if they weren't handicapped. The volunteers appreciated Christy's advice because it made them feel more able to help others. They learned how to put themselves in a handicapped person's place, and the advice helped them do a good job at the convention.

Christy won many scholarships and awards for her volunteering. One award she received was the Young Woman of the Year Scholarship. We believe she got these awards because she is the most dedicated person we've learned about.

Christy attends school at Georgia College in Milledgeville, Georgia. She has been going there for three years. She has an internship at her state capitol, and she loves being involved in politics. Christy really enjoys her political science and government courses, which are preparing her for law school. When she graduates from college, Christy plans to become a lawyer. She wants to stand up for people who have disabilities and make the world a better place for them.

Christy's college is a three-hour drive away from her family, so she does not get to visit them often. When she does get a chance to go home, her favorite thing to do is to take a walk in the country and listen to the sounds of nature.

Christy still enjoys dancing a lot.

Her favorite type of dance is ballet on pointe. This is a type of ballet in which the dancers wear ballet shoes with hard toes, so they can dance up high on their toes. Christy tries to practice one hour each day. She dances to relieve stress and pressure. She has danced many times for charity events. Christy sometimes dances in groups. She did a jazz dance at Super Bowl XXIX with a group of nine other girls from her college. They had to practice three hours each day for a week. When they were dancing, Christy said she felt excited and very proud. She always had to be prepared for the camera to be on her with all the world watching.

One way that Christy worked to make her personal dream come true was by entering the Miss Coastal Georgia beauty pageant. The whole week getting ready for the pageant was fun, and Christy made many new friends. They all worked very hard together and that made their friendships special. Christy really enjoyed being interviewed during the pageant. She had to answer questions and think of good answers. In one part of the contest, each girl had to show a special talent. For her talent performance, Christy danced ballet on pointe and she never looked better. When she got in the spotlight on stage and saw all the faces of the people in the audience, Christy felt very nervous and scared. Her hands felt sweaty and her legs were shaking. When the music started and the lights shined on her, she tried to think of this performance as just another practice. She took a deep breath and counted to ten. Her heart stopped pounding and she was ready to dance. That was one of Christy's favorite parts in the pageant. She danced ballet to country music and wore a sequined cowgirl hat. All the people clapped and cheered for her, especially the ones who knew her. Christy wore a very big smile. She loved the whole evening, and all through the night she felt so happy.

When the announcer said, "Christy Surrency is Miss Coastal Georgia!" Christy almost fell over! She couldn't believe the judges had chosen her. After that she held her head higher. Christy told us that participating in beauty pageants helped her to believe in herself. After being named Miss Coastal Georgia, Christy went on to compete in the Miss

*Christy accepts the Norman Vincent Peale Award in New York.*

Georgia America pageant. Later, she also won the Miss Macon pageant.

Christy once read the words of Lou Holtz, the Notre Dame football coach, "Life is ten percent what happens to you and 90 percent how you react to it." These words made a very big impression on Christy, and she tries to live by them each day. She believes you can make your life better if you follow this rule. Christy believes that everyone should learn to feel good about themselves, so she has written an educational program called Positively Reinforcing Ourselves (PRO), which teaches people about believing in themselves. Her message is to praise yourself when you do something good and learn from your mistakes. You should put a smile on your face and think positive. Christy hopes that schools will use her PRO guidelines to help children of all ages learn to love themselves and make our world a happier place.

Christy also begins every day with ten words that she says are the most powerful words that she knows, "I can do all things through Christ which strengthens me."

Christy is not only a hero in Georgia, but she is also a hero across the country too! In 1994 Christy won the Norman Vincent Peale Award for positive thinking. Only two people a year receive this honor. Other winners include former President Ronald Reagan and Elizabeth Dole, the head of the Red Cross. Christy was one of the youngest to get this award! Christy has already made such a positive difference in our world, we can't wait to see what she will do in the future!

## Here is a letter from Christy:

*It is positively amazing, absolutely astonishing, incredibly miraculous what you can become. This is the important message that I have been spreading throughout America. There are far too many people in this world that just do not believe in themselves. To me this is very sad. Personally, I have had to overcome many obstacles in my life and do not know how I could have done it without the power of positive thinking.*

*A positive attitude does not happen overnight or develop on its own. A positive attitude must be continuously worked on every day. However, I know that I have not developed this positive attitude on my own. I have always had three important influences throughout my life—God, family, and friends.*

*We all need to strive to become our best self and to always live our lives to the fullest. Always remember that we can do all things that we set our minds to. You can make a big difference in this world and "become what you want to be." Believe me, you can! Your life is exactly what you make of it. Every day we must positively reinforce ourselves. My challenge to you is to become the most positive and enthusiastic person you know.*

# MICHAEL CRISLER
*Friend of the Needy*

The world was truly blessed eight years ago when Michael Crisler was born. As a boy with Treacher Collins syndrome, life has not always been easy for Michael. Treacher Collins syndrome is a birth defect that has caused the bones in Michael's face to not grow right. He's already had five surgeries to correct his face. Michael also has a hearing aid to help him out because he doesn't exactly have all the parts to his ears. But none of these problems have slowed Michael down. His life is as busy as a bee's.

Since Michael was a small child, he's been raising money for many different causes. At three, he raised $500 for the Children's Miracle Network. Since then,

Michael has raised money for hospitals and different charities. Some of them are the Salvation Army, Children's Hospital, Muscular Dystrophy Association, Inter-Faith Task Force, Kops 'n' Kids, and others. He's also collected gifts like toys, bears, and hats for needy people. He used to go door-to-door asking for support, but now he says he gets most of his donations from car dealerships and other businesses in the Denver area.

When Michael heard about the Oklahoma City bombing in April 1996, he got really motivated. He told us, "I wanted to make a difference. I wanted to help them. I saw the picture of the fireman carrying the baby." Michael went through a lot of things to raise money for the victims. He went to the car dealerships, and he and his

*Michael's fund-raising efforts have paid off.*

Michael likes to do lots of other activities. He participates in a scouting program through his church, and he has lots of friends. If you think Michael is a fragile kid, you're wrong. At school, he likes to play tackle football, so he's pretty tough. He likes basketball, too, but he's still pretty short for the team. He also plays right wing for a soccer team called the Lion Kings.

Michael lives in Denver, Colorado, with his mother, Gayle, and his grandparents, Alva and Tom Munds. He and his family stay very busy during the holidays. Michael is the kind of kid who would rather spend his Thanksgiving serving food at shelters for the homeless. He enjoys making others happy, and he's got a heart of gold. Do you enjoy Christmas presents?

mother made flyers for a bowl-a-thon. Michael wanted to raise $20,000, but his mom thought that was too much so she talked him down to $10,000. Then, when she started sending out the flyers, she changed the amount to $5,000. Michael made her change it back. He felt he could help a lot more people with more money.

It turned out he had the right idea. The local and national media got ahold of the idea, and it wasn't long before Michael's phone was ringing like mad. People all over the country wanted to donate to the worthy cause. Michael raised more money for the unfortunate victims than any other single contributor. In the end, the grand total was nearly $37,000!

Besides fund-raising and bowling,

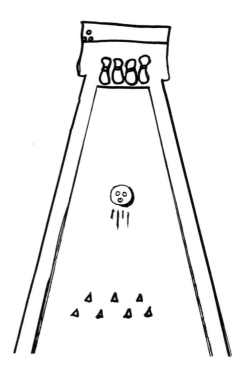

Michael didn't want any Christmas presents in 1996. He wanted to do what he did the year before. He planned to wrap them himself and give them away to unfortunate children. You might ask why he did it. He'd answer, "Because I feel like I have to. It's just the right thing to do." Michael likes to give so much that his church has set up a special fund called the Michael Crisler Fund for People in Need. This is so he can always have a supply of money to help others in need.

Michael has won many awards and honors for all his efforts to help others. The governor of Colorado asked Michael to help him carry the torch during the Olympic Festival in Colorado. He has been honored at his school with a special event called I Can Make a Difference Like Michael Day. His mom says their house is full of expensive prizes like TVs, VCRs, and stereos that were awarded to Michael for all his fund-raising. But it's hard to give Michael something he will keep because he's given away his prizes to needy people, too.

Michael has at least 12 surgeries to go before he's fully grown, so he still has many challenges ahead. He believes people should not think of him as a handicapped person because he has a birth defect. He doesn't think of himself as handicapped at all. If he's special at all, it's because he cares about others so much and he really wants to help them.

Altogether, Michael has raised more than $50,000 for different charities and special causes. But Michael always says, "I'm just like other kids," and he does these great things because it makes him feel good. He hopes others will learn to be nicer and care about others. Then, he thinks, we will have a better world.

# TWYLA RIVERS
## *Neighborhood Hero*

One Tuesday morning in April, everyone in math class at Columbine Elementary in Denver, Colorado, was watching the clock. Something special was about to happen. Finally the teacher dismissed the class. Forgetting the rules, the students ran to homeroom. The Channel 9 news camera team was already there. It was the most magnificent morning! Twyla Rivers, a student, had been chosen for the Channel 9 Kids Who Care Award. Twyla won this award because she is an amazing girl with many accomplishments.

Twyla lives with her great-grandparents and brother, Greg, on the east side of Denver. The family lives in a large old house with a red roof and a big backyard. Her great-grandparents have raised three generations of children in this house. All the neighbors are welcomed with open arms. When Twyla's friends visit, they like to play games and listen to rap music. Twyla's friends feel free to stop in for a chat with Great-Grandma anytime. She always makes the kids feel at home, even if Twyla is not there. Twyla is her great-grandparents' sparkling star and Energizer bunny all rolled into one black-haired, brown-eyed, dimpled, thirteen-year-old girl.

Twyla helps many people, and her great-grandpa is one of them. Twyla and her great-grandpa have a lot in common because they both have a sense of humor. They also worry about things. Twyla's great-grandpa has Parkinson's disease, an illness that happens late in life. It affects nerves, so

*Twyla doesn't hesitate to help others.*

people with this problem shake a lot and move slowly. Great-Grandpa has to take some special pills to control the disease. When he takes these pills, he sometimes has hallucinations. This means he hears and sees things that aren't really there. These pills also make him nervous, and he thinks about how something bad could be happening. Sometimes he thinks somebody is robbing the house or is in the backyard. Even if she is busy, Twyla will stop and help calm her great-grandpa. She helps him understand.

It is hard for Twyla's great-grandma. Sometimes she gets frustrated and impatient with her husband. Great-Grandma is glad to have Twyla around because she is patient and things are calmer when Twyla is there. Twyla's understanding and care for her great-grandpa helps her great-grandma get some much-needed rest.

Once, Great-Grandpa woke up at five in the morning. He shook Great-Grandma to wake her. He said, "The car is rolling down the street and it is not stopping!"

Great-Grandma yelled, "It's just your imagination, go back to sleep!" She was furious!

Twyla woke up with all the noise. She took Great-Grandpa to where the car was and said, "See, the car's right there." Finally Great-Grandpa calmed down and went back to sleep.

Another time, Great-Grandpa was walking down some stairs and began to shake. Twyla asked if he needed help. He said, "No," and he kept on walking. Then he slipped and fell, but he didn't get hurt. Twyla helped him back up the stairs and stayed with him so he wouldn't try to go down the stairs alone again.

Besides her great-grandparents, Twyla loves everything about her church. She goes with her aunt and her great-grandma to services every Sunday at the Good Shepherd Baptist Church. She feels welcome because she knows almost everyone. They look out for her and trust her. Twyla does lots of things at her church. Before church services, Twyla attends Sunday school. Sometimes the teacher is not there, so she takes control of the class. Twyla loves to read about and discuss Jesus Christ. On the third Sunday of every month, Twyla sings with a choir of children. On the fourth Sunday of every month, she ushers. Before the sermon, Twyla passes the basket to collect money to support her church.

Twyla, her aunt, and her great-grandma vacuum their church and wash the pastor's cups. Every other Saturday they dust the windows and the pews. Once a year, Twyla helps the church get a fresh coat of white paint. No matter how many other things

Twyla has to do, she finds time to help at church.

When Twyla attended Columbine Elementary School, she was in the gifted and talented program. It was called the Challenge Team. To get into the Challenge Team, you must score 80 percent or higher on a long series of tests. The teachers expect you to do better than average students. This class was made up of third, fourth, and fifth graders, and Twyla was part of the class through all these grades.

When Twyla started this group in the third grade, she was shy and quiet, but friendly. She would not speak out or volunteer. She has changed a lot. She volunteered for *News Team*, was a leader in the Student Council, and worked as a conflict manager.

*News Team* is a kids' news program that Twyla's class did every other Friday.

The program covers current news from around the world, national news, local news, weather, entertainment, specials, editorials, and sports. The class even made up their own commercials. Twyla volunteered for a variety of reporting jobs, but usually her hand would shoot high into the air when her teacher asked for an entertainment reporter. She began her report with, "Hello, my name is Twyla Rivers," and then she flashed her golden smile. Twyla talked about singers, music, and movies. She rattled off the top ten music groups. Sometimes Twyla would sing one of the top ten songs. Whenever Twyla sings, it only takes a minute and the audience is cheering for more.

One of her best friends, who was also in the Challenge Team, is Joe Ford. Twyla and Joe have been friends for years. Together they make a great team. They help each other, play together, and share ideas. Joe has cerebral palsy. Cerebral palsy is caused by damage to the brain, which makes it hard for Joe to move his muscles. This makes it difficult for Joe to talk. Twyla is best at communicating with Joe because she is a patient and understanding person. She listens carefully to Joe and then repeats what Joe says. When Twyla doesn't understand him, she doesn't get upset or angry. She just asks Joe to repeat what he said. She never makes him feel bad about his disability. Twyla jokes around with Joe and this makes him feel great. Once Twyla and Joe made up a crazy commercial about charcoal cookies for *News Team*. At the end of the commercial, everyone was laughing. Twyla loves sports and so does Joe. At recess they

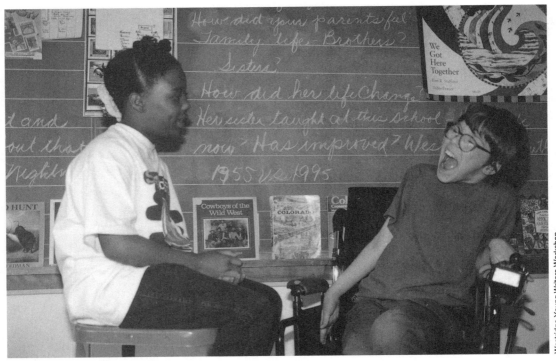

*Twyla laughs with Joe Ford.*

play tetherball and basketball. Twyla often thinks about her friendship with Joe. No matter what she has to do, she always finds time for him. They'll be friends for a long time.

Joe can't do some things, but this doesn't stop him from trying new things. Twyla and Joe both wanted to be president of the Student Council at Columbine. They were willing to take on the frustrating job of getting elected. All the candidates had to give speeches at two assemblies. At the first election assembly, Joe made his speech and a classmate repeated it for the audience. Then Twyla said her speech. At the second assembly, Twyla made a big decision. It was a precious moment for her.

Just before she made her speech, she asked the teacher if she could change it a little. The teacher said she could.

When Twyla stood before the student body in her dark green jumpsuit, her twinkling brown eyes shone with anticipation. She was nervous. What would everyone think of her change? She looked at her fellow candidates for confidence. They smiled at her. Twyla turned and faced the audience. The auditorium was quiet as the teachers and students patiently waited for her to begin. Suddenly Twyla's powerful voice filled the room with her song. She had the nerve and courage to sing her campaign speech! After her song, the teachers stood up and applauded Twyla for taking a risk and having the courage to be different. Twyla didn't win the election. She came in second. But, when she found out Joe would be president and she would be sergeant at arms, Twyla went wild!

Every Friday, Twyla and Joe gave up their lunch recess to attend Student Council meetings. As sergeant at arms, Twyla's job was to keep order during meetings and call on members for ideas. It was a very tough responsibility to keep order at the meetings, to make sure that her friend Joe was understood, and to keep track of all the sales orders, but Twyla did it all. Twyla also visited classrooms to sell suckers and talk about the canned food drive. She worked on the school dances, T-shirt sales, and other activities that the council sponsored.

Twyla doesn't care if people think she's a tomboy because she does what she enjoys. At recess, Twyla plays double-dutch jump rope (with two ropes) until her feet hurt. On Field Day, Twyla walked away with a fistfull of first-place ribbons. She entered the most complicated events. With a smile on her face, she tackled the relay, the long jump, and the softball throw with no problem. She made it look easy.

On Wednesdays during lunch recess, you would see Twyla in her royal purple T-shirt. This special T-shirt meant that she was a Columbine School conflict manager. Twyla was responsible for taking care of her T-shirt. She kept it neat and clean. When she wore that shirt, she was on duty. Twyla had to help solve conflicts on the playground and around school.

One day Twyla saw two students pushing each other. Calmly, she walked over to the basketball court. She listened to each person's story and took notes on a form. The students acted like they were still angry. Twyla didn't get pulled into the conflict. She did not take sides. She was very honest and showed a lot of self control. Suddenly, the students started punching each other. Twyla saw that she needed some help with this conflict, so she asked a teacher to help. She didn't let her ego get in the way of asking for help to solve the problem. Twyla's conflict training and good sportsmanship are useful in conflict management. Her sense of humor also helps her solve some challenging situations. Once,

when on duty, Twyla said, "We should get paid for doing this much work!" Of course, she was joking.

Twyla likes to go to the Red Shield Center after school. It is a Christian recreation center where kids and teenagers go when they are bored. They have organized games, an arcade, and basketball and drill teams. Twyla has taken part in the Red Shield drill teams. Members on the drill teams clap their hands and stomp their feet to a certain beat. The kids and their leader, Francis Stone, make up most of the drills. The drill teams perform at places like the Holiday Inn.

Twyla has also played on an all-girl basketball team at the Red Shield Center. She is a good shooter, and she would set up her teammates with shots. She was an above average point guard and was dedicated to her team. She never missed a practice, even if she was tired or a little sick. She worked out by doing a lot of hard running exercises, which she calls sprints, suicides, or bone crushers. When someone remarked that her team had won only one game, she flashed her golden smile and said, "It's better than nothing." Now that Twyla is at Morey Junior High, she's still playing basketball and she enjoys playing music, too.

During the summer, her family loves to go on an annual camping trip to Cherry Creek Park. They pack food, tents, and their relatives into three cars and off they go. Every year Great-Grandma worries that the old truck won't make it, but somehow it always does. The camping trip is a good time for eating and sharing family stories about their relatives when they were young. Great-Grandma, who grew up on a farm in Akron, Colorado, tells about Bill Pickett. He was a famous African American cowboy. Twyla feels thankful she has a great-grandma who does so much for her family.

Even though Twyla is just a seventh-grader, her warm, friendly, confident smile tells you she can do it all! She's still working above her grade level in school, and now she's in a program called High Stride. This program helps kids prepare for college. Twyla is a role model, a friend, and a helper. Truly, Twyla Rivers is a kid who cares.

### Here is a letter from Twyla:

*When I was really little I used to say, "I can't." Now I don't believe in the word "can't" because I can. Don't ever say you can't, because you can. If you say you can't then you won't succeed. If you say you can, and you keep trying hard, then you WILL succeed.*

*If you really want to help people, you don't have to look very far. I have found that the people around me are the ones who need help the most. I like knowing the people I help, and I can see how much I am really making a difference. You may not have someone in your family who needs help, but you can always look for them at your school or church. Every school has someone who needs a friend. Helping others has made me feel good about myself.*

# EMILY GREBLE
*Super Volunteer*

Do you like to go to big parties, eat great food at barbecues, and dance to your favorite music? We sure do. Did you know becoming a volunteer can mean doing more of your favorite things all the time? We didn't until we met Emily Greble.

When Emily Greble was 15, she and a friend started a group called Youth-Grow. This organization helped high school students volunteer. The group's main goal was to work with adults that were mentally disabled. Youth-Grow put together special trips and events that got people with disabilities out of their group homes and into the community. The group set up barbecues, hiking trips, and dances. These events helped all the people meet others and have a good time. The high school kids enjoyed helping out, and the adults enjoyed getting out and being part of the community.

Emily Greble was the right person to start a high school volunteering group because she has lots of experience with volunteering. Emily started to volunteer when she was eight years old. She was scared at first, but now she looks forward to any chance she can to help others. She ran special programs for the Westchester Association of Retarded Citizens. She staffed the phones at phone-a-thons for Volunteers of America (VOA). She worked with the little kids at the YMCA. She planned pumpkin decorating events to raise money for the Cerebral Palsy Association of Westchester. She livened up young patients' days by

Greble family

*Emily Greble*

to order a hot dog and then not have hot dogs for them.

Emily was really nervous about the big event. To make matters worse, when the day finally arrived, it rained all day. Some people wanted to cancel the celebration, but Emily knew it was important to go on. What made Emily keep going were all the smiles on all the people's faces. Emily told us, "It was the hardest day of my life. I was really lucky because my dad woke up at 4:00 a.m. to drive me over to the field. He stayed all morning to help me hammer stakes in the ground for the tents and move some of the heavy equipment. I couldn't have done it without him." Emily worried that she had done a bad job. When they called her back the next year to run the Special Olympics, she knew they liked her work and she was glad to volunteer again.

After two years of running the Special Olympics, Emily Greble won the Westchester County Department of Mental Heath Volunteer of the Year Award. She was the youngest person to ever receive this award. She received it for a number of reasons. First, she ran the Special Olympics so well. Second, the group was proud of her work helping out with group homes. These are homes that have a few counselors to help adults who have disabilities. The homes are set up to give these adults a chance to live on their own. The third reason Emily received the award was for teaching a Sunday school class to children with disabilities. To help these children, Emily invited kids from the regular classes to join in so they could all learn together. With all of Emily's work, she has won many awards

visiting them at Blythedale Children's Hospital. You name it, Emily has done it. No matter what Emily does, she does it with a smile on her face. (A big smile to be exact!)

Emily shared one of the most challenging jobs she has ever accepted as a volunteer. When Emily was 14 years old, she was in charge of the Westchester-Putnam Special Olympics, which is like a field day for children with disabilities. Emily organized about a thousand people. She had to tell them where they were supposed to be and what they were supposed to do. Emily had to get all the materials for the events, the food, the tents, and the people to help. Emily worked hard because she sure didn't want a long line of people waiting

and learned a very important lesson for her life. Volunteering not only helps others, but it has also helped her.

Emily Greble was born on January 7, 1978. It was a cold, blustery day during an ice storm on Long Island, not far from New York City. Emily was supposed to be born on December 10, 1977, but she wasn't ready. Emily's mom says that she was stubborn then and still is at times.

Emily lived in Glen Cove, New York, for a few years. When Emily was two, her brother Matthew was born. Shortly after his birth, the family found out that Matthew had cerebral palsy, which means his brain does not work the way most people's brains do. Matthew's life is different from Emily's. He needs a lot of help to live. He can't talk and he uses a wheelchair. He needs help eating and getting dressed. Emily told us that Matthew is probably one of the happiest kids alive. He's always smiling and loves to be involved with activities such as bowling, horseback riding, and music. Emily knows that having Matthew for her brother has made her life better. Through helping Matthew, Emily has learned that helping is good and it makes her feel happy.

Emily remembers that it was great living in her first home in Glen Cove. This was one of the few areas in the county where people spoke more than one language. In her community, people spoke Italian and English or Spanish and English. A lot of people who lived there didn't have much money. Emily used to invite friends over from her class for dinner. Sometimes her friends would ask if they could bring their brothers or sisters too, because they might not get to eat that night otherwise. So, Emily's house was always full of visitors. Her mom was good at stretching meals to feed all who came.

Glen Cove was far away from her dad's work. And, as Matthew got older, the family's split-level house was not good for his wheelchair. So the family moved to Chappaqua, New York. Emily felt a little sad when her family decided to move. Emily's family continued helping others in their new community. They felt that helping others was important, and her mom

spent most of her time volunteering. Sometimes Emily went along. Emily saw what her mom was doing and thought it was pretty cool. This is how Emily got into volunteering and how she learned that all people should have an equal chance to do everything. Because of her brother's disability and her mother's efforts to help the disabled, Emily has set a goal to improve the lives of the people she works with.

You may think Emily spends all her time volunteering. Well, that isn't true. She is a normal kid who loves to laugh and hang out with her friends. Theater is one of her passions in life. She not only

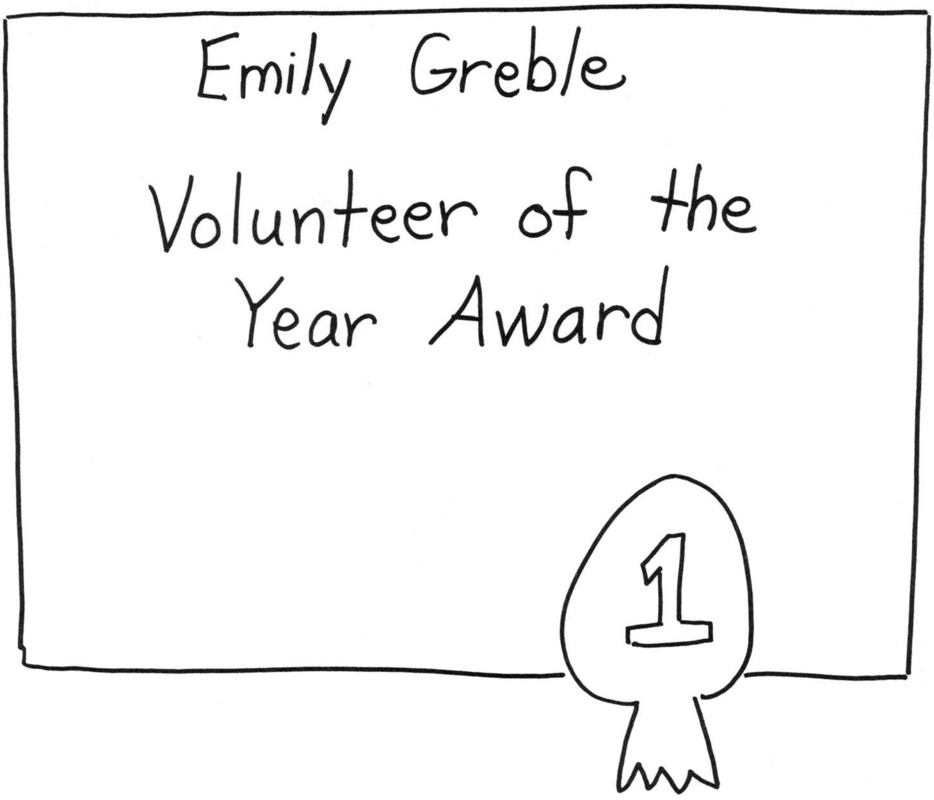

Emily Greble

Volunteer of the Year Award

likes doing performances, but she likes working backstage too. During high school, she was involved in many aspects of theater. In her freshman year, she worked backstage and did publicity for the play, *Little Shop of Horrors*. She and a friend wrote their own musical with 17 songs in it. Emily directed their play when it was performed at school.

Emily really loves to sing. At home, she sings all the time and drives her family crazy. They would ask, "Would you be quiet for at least one minute?" Emily likes to perform anyplace. She even sings at funerals. She really loves performing and hopes to be on Broadway someday. She knows that getting into acting is difficult, and she will probably have to spend a lot of time doing odd jobs. She told us that's why she sets the table and serves the food at home—because a lot of actresses are waitresses and she is practicing already!

Now that Emily is at the College of William and Mary in Virginia, she is still involved with the theater, singing, and volunteering. She sings with a group that does free programs in her area. Her sorority is helping to raise money to fight child abuse, and they work with a children's hospital raising money and doing projects to help the sick children. She's also helping a middle-aged woman with Down's syndrome "just for myself," she says.

Emily doesn't have to volunteer, but she does. She is a great person and she puts a smile on everybody's face. If everyone in the world was more like Emily, there would be no such thing as sadness.

## Emily Greble shared this message with us:

*You live only once, so you have to make the best of it. You should be kind to others around you. You shouldn't make fun of others if they learn more slowly than everybody else because that is how they were born. There are many ways to make a difference. You can say hello to someone who's lonely, help older people get their groceries, or maybe help your friends who are a little slow with their work. I decided I would be like my mom and really make a difference in this world.*

# EDWARD SANTOS
## *Helping Things Grow*

If you visited lower Manhattan on a spring day, you might be surprised to find so many people working in such pretty gardens. Once these gardens were trashed-out lots where drug dealers and gangs hung out. When Edward Santos had the chance to help make a garden out of nothing, he took it. Soon, others started getting involved and volunteering, and it didn't take long to turn things around in their neighborhood.

Edward's neighborhood in New York used to be a lot tougher. He lives in lower Manhattan with his mother, Leoncia, his older brother, Victor, and his sister, Lili. In their neighborhood there was always yelling and fighting going on. There was no safe place that kids could play because of all the problems. It would have been easy for Edward and his older brother to get into trouble, but their mother kept them busy doing active things. Edward's hero is his mother because she has raised him and his siblings very well all by herself. His family likes to go to parks, zoos, and museums.

Since the gardens were made, there haven't been as many scary things happening in Edward's neighborhood, and there haven't been as many problems. It all began one day when Edward was just nine years old. He was walking down the street, and he saw a man named Normand Vallee picking up trash. Edward asked the man why he was cleaning up the empty lot. Normand told him he was going to make a

Santos family

*Edward is proud of his gardens.*

They also worked on other lots, and pretty soon they had three gorgeous gardens. They are named Green Oasis, Gilbert's Sculpture, and the Fireman's Memorial Garden. They planted and built new things inside them. Edward worked very hard. He helped lay the foundation for a gazebo and an outdoor theater. He put in a marble rock path, and he helped with the planting. The gardens have cherry trees, evergreens, flowers, vegetables, grass, and almost everything you can think of!

One hard job for Edward happened when he was just 12 years old. He was put in charge of a group of older workers. It seemed strange to Edward to be telling older people what to do, but Edward showed them how to garden just fine. Edward has always really enjoyed taking visitors on tours of the gardens and showing them all the things that have changed. He is very proud of all his hard work and the work of his neighbors. Now people enjoy eating the vegetables, sitting in the gazebo, or watching entertainment at the outdoor theater.

There have been times when the neighbors didn't know if the gardens would continue, but somehow they've managed with Edward's help. He's helped to raise money by working at a street festival in his neighborhood each summer. Edward has been such an important part of the garden project that, when he was 17, he got the Mayor's Youth Award for all his hard work and his other volunteer activities. Edward also got a special award from the Giraffe Project. He was one of the lucky young Giraffe Project kids who went to Moscow to meet with Russian youth.

garden out of the lot, which is owned by the Green Thumb Project. Edward decided he wanted to make a difference, too, so he got down on his hands and knees and he started cleaning. Later, Edward got his brother and his friend Mars to help. They all started working in the garden every summer day instead of playing or getting into trouble.

Edward still enjoys working in the gardens and giving tours. He's been working with the New York Restoration Project and Americorps, fixing up Fort Tryon Park. He's also working on another garden called What Nature Intended. This is an educational garden where he's helping teach young children about gardening and nature. He's also on the Board of Directors for the garden named Green Oasis. Altogether, he's worked on a total of eight gardens. He also has a two-year college degree, and he wants to get another college degree in some kind of computer studies.

We think Edward is a hero because he made a big difference in his own life and the life of his neighborhood. A hero doesn't have to save someone's life. This hero has shown us that a big heart can make a big difference in even a little part of the world.

## Edward shared this message with us:

*Volunteering can do many things to change your life. I learned that I could make a difference in my neighborhood. Through the gardens, my street was a happier and safer place to be. I also gained a lot of confidence and kept myself busy and out of trouble. Even though I was young when I started working in the gardens, my efforts helped get many others involved and made a great change in my neighborhood.*

# SARAH SWAGART
## *Improving the Community*

You can't judge a book by its cover. This saying means that even though something looks bad on the outside, it might be wonderful inside. The opposite can be true, too. Even though something looks great on the outside, it might really be a living nightmare. This was true of the street where Sarah Swagart lived. It was called Happy Lane.

Everything seemed fine on Happy Lane in Whidbey Island, Washington. Sarah lived with her parents, Dave and Cindy. She also has an older brother named Nate. When Sarah was seven years old, a very bad thing began happening to her. Even though the neighbor boy looked nice, he started sexually abusing Sarah. This went on until Sarah was 12 years old, but she was afraid to tell anybody about it. After a while, she couldn't handle the terrible secret she'd been keeping anymore. When she was a teenager, she turned her life over to drugs and alcohol.

Sarah, as you can imagine, wasn't very pleasant to live with. Her parents knew she needed help and she needed it fast. They decided to admit her to a mental hospital and a drug treatment facility. She was in and out of these places for years. She dropped out of school because the neighbor boy started following her around wherever she went. Sarah spent years getting better, and now she is very thankful for all the people who helped her. She is especially thankful to her parents for getting her the help she needed.

Swagart family

*Sarah tried skateboarding just once, when she was small.*

One thing that has really helped Sarah get better was taking on a big community project. Several of Sarah's friends were skateboarders who were always getting hassled about where they skated. James Walker, one of Sarah's friends, was skating in a parking lot and he got a ticket. He faced a $500 fine, 90 days in jail, and 20 hours of community service.

Sarah was very frustrated, puzzled, and angry about this. The community thought the skaters were troublemakers. Sarah said, "Sure, they looked weird and everything, but I knew they were really good guys. They were just doing the sport that they love." The skaters looked like

drug addicts, punks, and freaks, but Sarah knew them better, and she knew they were wonderful inside.

Even though Sarah doesn't skate, she decided she wanted to do something to help the skaters. Sarah gathered her thoughts, then she talked with her parents and her counselor about building a skateboard park. They said she had their full support.

Sarah soon learned that she needed a petition as part of her ammunition. She and her skater friends started taking the petition all through their community—to football games, businesses, and workplaces. Sarah and her friends also walked door-to-door getting signatures. She walked all around town with the petition. We bet she burned a lot of calories!

After months and months, all their hard work paid off. Sarah took herself, a delegation of friends, and about 300 signatures to the mayor. Sarah was afraid to speak in public, so she was very nervous. She knew that she'd have to get over her fear. She couldn't let clammy hands and shaky knees get in her way.

Sarah used her ammunition to load her gun, then she fired this argument: the soccer players have soccer fields, the baseball players have baseball fields, the football players have football fields, and the ice skaters even have skating rinks, so why can't skateboarders have a place to practice their sport?

After Sarah spoke, the mayor understood the problem better. He asked Sarah to do some research on a park and come back with some solid plans. It was a big job, but Sarah said, "I've been very confident about this project from the beginning."

Sarah began the first skaters' group in town, called Nobody Special. They started getting involved in many community events and performances. They walked in several parades, did skating demonstrations, and ran booths at local fairs to educate the public about their sport.

The next time Sarah and her friends saw the mayor, they had a whole bunch of information to share with him. They had gathered information about skateboard parks around the country so they would know what kinds of problems they had and what worked. They had an architect build a model of a skateboard park to show what it would look like. Sarah worked very hard to get the mayor to approve her project.

The mayor had some new information for Sarah, too. He said he was impressed with the image the skaters had been showing to others. There were less complaints about them, and the public's opinion of them had been raised. He said he still liked Sarah's idea, and he had already picked out a piece of land where the new park could be built. Now Sarah would have to make the park fit in the space, deal with the neighbors' concerns, and raise the money.

Sarah and her friends found solutions to these problems. She met with the neighbors and talked to them about loud music, lights, and parking. They also met with the architect again to make a few changes. That only left the money.

Many places have offered to contribute their money and supplies to help build the park. It will cost about $170,000. Sarah and the Nobody Special group have had to come up with a lot of money on their own already. They have had car washes, garage sales, raffles, information booths, and different fund-raisers. They

Swagart family

*Sarah shows off a model of the skateboarders' park.*

haven't reached their goal just yet, but Sarah says, "I've never given up on these skaters. I don't think I'll ever give up." Today Sarah has another thing going for her. She believes in herself.

Sarah is still raising money for the skateboard park. She's also taking courses through a local college to get her GED, which is equal to a high school diploma.

She has big plans to go to college in the future. She wants to be an art therapist who works with abused children.

Sarah shares this message in her speeches: "You're less likely to sell a bag of fruit if you're whispering down a well than if you're standing on top of a tree and yelling it. It's really true and that's just what I've had to do."

# OUR VISION FOR A BETTER TOMORROW

You have just read the stories of some young people who have helped others. Many of these kids are like you in many ways. Some of them saw something that needed to be done, some helped themselves through tough problems, others got involved with their families, and still others decided they wanted to do something for someone else. We believe there is so much to learn by helping others. We want to share what we have learned from these young people.

**Teddy Andrews** started making a difference in politics when he was only seven years old, by working for a man running for City Council. He started an organization that got other kids involved in volunteering.

**Ashley Black** saw something she felt strongly about on TV. She helped others see that games are not fun when they show disrespect to others. She got many people involved in changing the laws of her state.

**Renata Bradford** uses her sense of humor in all she does. She has battled cancer and has given hope to others fighting this disease. She has taught us not to judge others by the way they look. She showed us to treat people with illnesses just like everyone else.

**Michael Crisler** is small. He's also very young. He even has a birth defect. But

Michael has proven that no matter how old or small you are, you can make a giant effort to help others. He's raised more money than some whole companies have raised to help the needy.

**Emily Greble** decided to use her talent to help people with disabilities. She searched around her community for organizations that supported people with disabilities, and she has touched the lives of many with her special charm.

**Kory Johnson** taught us that kids are often the best people to stand up for other kids. We know from Kory that adults don't always know exactly what a kid needs, so we have to tell them in big and important ways.

**David Levitt** found his cause in an ordinary place: the newspaper. He worked hard collecting food for the needy and getting his School Board to contribute leftover food to feed homeless people. His program has grown a lot from such a simple idea.

**Iqbal Masih** taught us that all children are precious. We all deserve to laugh, play, and act like kids. His message helped to free many other slave children, and his short life was an important lesson for everyone to help stop child slavery.

**Melissa Poe** didn't stop with the president. She showed us that a kid's message can be heard by even more important people. Sometimes the biggest concerns and actions for the planet come from kids.

**The Quincy Kids** showed the whole world how to take charge and make a dream come true. They showed us that a group of dedicated students can make a big difference, even in another part of our world.

**Twyla Rivers** has the heart of an angel and the energy of an Energizer bunny. Twyla taught us that even a ten-year-old can find many ways to help people right in her own neighborhood.

**Cari Rons** helped us realize that some heroes have to start by helping themselves through the challenges that life throws at them. Life is not easy, but with an attitude like Cari's that says, "I just won't give up," we can get through the tough times.

**Jim Stuart Runner-Beuning** found that there are so many people with talent that he started an international organization to recognize and thank people who do things for others. He taught us that even a kid can make a big difference by starting a group like Kids Who Care.

**Edward Santos** helped create beauty in an area that had a lot of crime. His neighborhood now has beautiful gardens, and Edward has grown into a fine young man. He showed us that hard work really pays.

**Brianne Schwantes'** life is sometimes very hard. She has decided how she can make the best of having brittle bone disease, and she has started a national newsletter to help other young people with this disease.

**Christy Surrency** has shown us how important it is to have a positive attitude and great self-esteem. She has turned her own disability into one of her greatest assets. She also shows other people how to create positive changes in their own lives.

**Sarah Swagart** helped us remember that you can't judge a book by its cover. You have to look under the surface to find the real thing. If you have faith in yourself, working for a hard goal can be just as much of a reward as reaching it.

**Charlie Wolfe** learned to get his anger out in poetry. He has helped others learn to write poetry to express their anger, and he has worked to keep kids in school and out of trouble. Along the way Charlie found out that he wants to work helping others for his career.

We hope that you will think about making volunteering a part of your life. Give it a try. You may find you grow and learn so much that it will change your life. If it doesn't work out the first time, try again. Remember, every little bit helps. Just like these young heroes, the actions you take will make a difference in the world around you.

# GETTING INVOLVED

Now that you have heard how so many other young people have made a difference in their community, it's your turn to try. In this part of our book, we want to share ideas about how you can get involved. Working to help your community makes you feel stronger and better about yourself. It doesn't require any special skills. It is a great way to get out, meet new people, and experience new things. When you volunteer you can get involved in community projects or just help the people around you.

Once you are ready to begin, here are some questions you might want to ask yourself. Your answers to these questions will guide you in finding the ways you will most enjoy helping others.

## WHAT THINGS INTEREST ME?

When you get started with volunteering, it is important to choose something that you like. If you don't like working with sick people, don't volunteer in hospitals. If you like animals, call your local zoo or animal adoption agencies. If you have a talent like singing or writing poetry, you can share your time in nursing homes or hospitals. If you like to work outside, there are many environmental causes you can join. You can even go through your neighborhoods and volunteer to help elderly people with their yard work. The most important thing to remember is that you need to choose something that you can enjoy and that you will stick with.

## DO I WANT TO VOLUNTEER TO HELP PEOPLE, ANIMALS, OR THE ENVIRONMENT?

A lot of people forget that volunteering can involve things besides working with people. There are many opportunities to help with animals and the environment. If you like to be outdoors you can volunteer to work at parks or neighborhood cleanups, or even fixing up lakes and ponds. You can also look around for local animal shelters or veterinarians who need help caring for and cleaning up after the animals. Remember, there are many worldwide organizations that are working to protect people, animals, and places.

## DO I WANT TO HELP A GROUP OF PEOPLE OR AN INDIVIDUAL?

There are many ways to help individual people. If you like a subject in school, you can volunteer to tutor other kids. A lot of schools need students to help disabled kids

get from class to class or to help with their assignments. You might even find a person in your neighborhood who needs help getting groceries.

If you prefer to work with many people, there are lots of ways to help groups. You can go to senior citizen homes, hospitals, day care centers, or recreation centers. Just look for any place with a lot of people and ask if they need help.

If you volunteer at a center or a hospital where there are lots of different people all the time, then you'll meet more people, all of whom may be very different. This can be rewarding because you'll learn about all kinds of people. It also means that every time you go in, there will always be someone to help. Volunteering for both groups and individuals can be a rewarding, building experience.

## DO I WANT TO WORK BY MYSELF, WITH A FRIEND, OR WITH AN ORGANIZATION?

Think really hard about this one. Decide whether you can work by yourself or if you prefer to work with others. Some people feel more comfortable working independently. Some people like to choose by themselves what they will do, where they will go, and who they will help.

Some people think volunteering is more fun when you work with a friend. A friend may get you motivated to start and give you company while you work. You can choose the things you both have in common. You also have each other to talk to about your volunteering.

Volunteer groups often send their workers to jobs that involve working with different people and going to different places. The groups' tasks may already be planned, so you don't have to find your own. The group also can help train you for different jobs. Working with a group helps you meet new people that like to do the same things you do. It is a great way to get to know others and have new experiences.

## DO I WANT TO START MY OWN GROUP?

Starting your own group can be a little tougher, but if you form a group of people who have the same goals, it can be the most

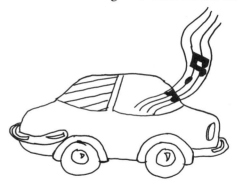

rewarding thing you've done. Remember, organizing your project is going to be very important in getting your plans off to a great start. Here are some things to think about before you start your own volunteer group:

1. Find a cause that you feel very strongly about. Remember, if you are going to motivate yourself and others, you've got to believe in what you are doing.
2. Talk to everybody you know. Find out what they think about the cause. Try to get people involved with you. Find out what has already been done and talk to the people who did it.
3. Start getting people together to brainstorm ideas. Remember, everyone in the group can bring great ideas to the project. The more stuff people contribute, the more willing they are to work. Everyone needs to be involved and no one wants to be bossed around.
4. Keep gathering information about your cause. Don't be afraid to write or call your local governmental officials. Senators, representatives, mayors, and city council officials may be able to help you get more information and help shape your ideas.
5. Keep checking your goals. Remember, you may hit a problem and need to fix your plans as you go along.
6. Ask your group to help decide what to do and how to do it. Keep plugging along and don't be afraid to go back and do the earlier steps more than once.

Creating your own organization takes a lot of planning, people, and time, but you will be helping people, animals, or the environment. Like the young people in our book, you will help others and help yourself. It is a challenge worth tackling.

## FINDING A PLACE TO GET INVOLVED

In the next chapter, you will find information that will help you get in touch with organizations that need your support. You'll find two lists. The first is a list of national volunteer headquarters that have offices all across the United States. You can call the national number or check for the group's name in your local phone directory. Ask the person at the national office to give you the telephone number of the group's office in your city. Remember, long-distance numbers that start with 800 don't cost you or your parents any money.

The second list is a state-by-state resource guide of organizations that might need your help. If the organization doesn't have any opportunities available now for kids, be sure to ask the person who answers the phone if he or she knows who might need help from a super kid like you.

And, if you have a great idea for starting your own program, ask the person if their organization would like to be a part of your big plan!

If these lists don't help you get started, you can still find lots of places where you can make a difference. There are many ways that you can help the environment, wildlife, homeless and hungry people, disabled people, victims of natural disasters, plus many more. You can help in your neighborhood, city, state, country, or any other part of the world. You can try looking in the yellow pages under "Associations," "Clubs," and "Social Service Organizations." Also, read your local newspaper. Many organizations are featured that need volunteers. The articles usually give a number to call or a place to go. Look for opportunities through your church or school. You can ask friends and family if they know of any places that need your time and energy. You can also ask the librarian for help.

It won't be difficult to get involved and start helping others. Whatever you do, don't be afraid to ask other people to help you get involved. Remember, you have special talents to share with others, and many people need your help!

# RESOURCE GUIDE

## NATIONAL HEAD-QUARTERS OF PLACES WHERE YOU CAN HELP

**American Association of Retired Persons (AARP)**
1909 K Street NW
Washington, DC 20049
(202) 662-4895
Helps the elderly

**American Red Cross**
431 18th Street NW
Washington, DC 20006
(202) 737-8300
Helps victims of disasters

**Big Brothers/Big Sisters of America**
230 N. 13th Street
Philadelphia, PA 19107
(215) 567-7000
A program for older kids to get involved with younger kids

**Boys and Girls Clubs of America**
1230 West Peachtree Street
Atlanta, GA 30309
(404) 815-5700
A positive way for kids to join youth clubs

**Boy Scouts of America**
1325 W. Walnut Hill Lane
P.O. Box 152079
Irving, TX 75015
(214) 580-2000
National headquarters of the Boy and Eagle Scouts

**City Cares of America**
1737 H Street NW
Washington, DC 20006
(202) 887-0500
Community service group projects

**Civitan International**
1 Civitan Place
Birmingham, AL 35213-1983
(205) 591-8910
(800) CIVITAN
Helps people become good citizens

**Giraffe Project**
197 Second Street
P.O. Box 759
Langley, WA 98260
(206) 221-7989
Recognizes people of all ages who "stick their necks out" to make a difference. You can nominate someone special for an award.

**Girl Scouts of the U.S.A**
420 5th Avenue
New York, NY 10018
(212) 852-8000
National headquarters of the Girl Scouts

**Goodwill Industries of America**
9200 Wisconsin Avenue
Bethesda, MD 20814
(310) 530-6500
Helps needy people

**Greenpeace U.S.A.**
1432 U Street NW
Washington, DC 20009
(202) 462-1177
Helps animals and the
environment all over the
world

**Habitat for Humanity**
121 Habitat Street
Americus, GA
31709-3498
(912) 924-6935
Builds homes for needy
people

**Junior Chamber
International**
400 University Drive
Coral Gables, FL 33134
(305) 446-7608
Helps people become good
leaders by helping their
communities

**Junior Optimist Clubs**
4494 Lindell Boulevard
St. Louis, MO 63108
(314) 371-6000
Helps girls in sixth
through ninth grades and
all kids in seventh through
twelfth grades become
great citizens

**Key Club**
3636 Woodview Trace
Indianapolis, IN
46268-3196
(317) 875-8755
Gets kids in grades six and
above into great service
positions

**Keyette International**
1421 Kalmia Road NW
Washington, DC 20012
(202) 726-4619
A service club for girls in
grades nine through twelve

**Kids FACE** (For a Clean
Environment)
P.O. Box 158254
Nashville, TN 37215
(800) 952-3223
An international group
with thousands of mem-
bers who care about the
environment

**Kiwanis International**
3636 Woodview Trace
Indianapolis, IN
46268-3196
(317) 875-8755
(800) 549-2647
Runs lots of programs to
help people of all ages

**La Sertoma International**
12612 W. 101st Street
Lenexa, KS 66215
(913) 492-3116
A club of people who are
interested in community
service

**Make-A-Wish Foundation**
100 West Clarendon,
Suite 2200
Phoenix, AZ 85013
(602) 279-9474
(800) 722-9474
Makes needy kids' wishes
come true

**Muscular Dystrophy
Association**
3300 East Sunrise Drive
Tucson, AZ 85718
(520) 529-2000
Raises money and has pro-
grams for people with MD

**National Assistance
League**
5627 Fernwood Avenue
Los Angeles, CA 90028
(213) 469-5897
Dedicated to helping all
people in need

**National Youth Leadership
Council**
1910 West County Road B
Roseville, MN 55113
(612) 631-3672
Trains youth in service

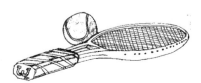

**NGA, Inc.**
1007-B Street Road
Southampton, PA 18966
(215) 322-5759
Gives new clothes and
linens to needy families

**Pilot International**
244 College Street
P.O. Box 4844
Macon, GA 31213-0599
(912) 743-7403
Sponsors Anchor Clubs,
run through schools, for
kids interested in service

**Points of Light Foundation**
1737 H Street NW
Washington, DC 20006
(202) 223-9186
(800) 879-5400
Helps young people get
involved with their com-
munities and solve serious
problems

**Salvation Army National
Headquarters**
615 Slaters Lane
P.O. Box 269
Alexandria, VA 22313
(703) 684-5500
Has programs to help
needy people

**Soroptimist International
of the Americas**
1616 Walnut Street,
Suite 700
Philadelphia, PA 19103
(215) 732-0512
Sponsors "S" Clubs for
high school students interested in service

**United Nations Children's
Fund (UNICEF)**
3 United Nations Plaza
New York, NY 10017
(212) 326-7000
(212) 702-7100
Helps children throughout
the world

**United Way of America**
701 N. Fairfax Street
Alexandria, VA
22314-2045
(703) 836-7100
Runs many programs for
community service across
America

**U.S.A. Harvest**
(800) 872-4366
Gathers food and gives it
to the homeless in 23
states

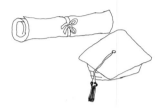

**Volunteers of America**
3939 N. Causeway
Boulevard
Metairie, LA 70002
(504) 837-2652
(800) 899-0089
Runs a variety of charities
and service programs

**YES! (Youth for Environ-
mental Sanity)**
706 Frederick Street
Santa Cruz, CA 95062
(408) 459-9344
Runs programs and sum-
mer camps for kids who
want to help the environ-
ment

**Youth Service America**
1101 15th Street NW,
Suite 200
Washington, DC 20004
(202) 296-2992
Promotes and creates
youth service programs
across the United States

**Youth Volunteer Corps of America**
6310 Lamar Avenue,
Suite 125
Overland Park, KS 66202
(913) 423-9822
Creates service projects for
kids age 11 to 18

**Young Men's Christian Associations of the U.S.A. (YMCA U.S.A. )**
101 N. Wacker Drive
Chicago IL 60606
(312) 977-0031
Has lots of different programs for kids

## STATE BY STATE GUIDE TO ORGANIZATIONS WHERE YOU CAN MAKE A DIFFERENCE

### ALABAMA
**Civitan International**
1 Civitan Place
Birmingham, AL
35213-1983
(205) 591-8910
1 (800) CIVITAN

**Volunteers of America**
Birmingham
(800) 859-4431
Huntsville (205) 830-2155
Mobile (334) 666-4431
Montgomery
(800) 859-4431

### ALASKA
**Kids Who Care**
c/o Jim Runner-Beuning
P.O. Box 60772
Fairbanks, AK
99706-0772

**Volunteers of America**
Anchorage
(907) 279-9634

### ARIZONA
**Children for a Safe Environment**
517 East Roanoke #A
Phoenix, AZ 85004
(602) 279-5001

**Make-A-Wish Foundation**
100 West Clarendon,
Suite 2200
Phoenix, AZ 85013
(602) 279-9474
(800) 722-9474

**Muscular Dystrophy Association**
3300 East Sunrise Drive
Tucson, AZ 85718
(520) 529-2000

**Student Environmental Action Coalition**
P.O. Box 248
Tucson, AZ 85702
(520) 903-0128

### ARKANSAS
**Mays Mission for the Handicapped**
604 Colonial Drive
Heritage Heights
Heber Springs, AR 72543
(501) 362-7526

**Volunteers of America**
Little Rock
(501) 374-1713

### CALIFORNIA
**Earth 2000**
P.O. Box 24, Dept. R
Shillington, PA 19607

**Earth Day Resources**
116 New Montgomery,
No. 530
San Francisco, CA 94105
(415) 495-5987
(800) 727-8619

**National Assistance League**
5627 Fernwood Avenue
Santa Cruz, CA 95062
(408) 459-9344

**Youth for Environmental Sanity (YES!)**
706 Frederick Street
Santa Cruz, CA 95062
(408) 459-9344

**Volunteers of America**
Los Angeles
(213) 389-1500
Sacramento
(916) 442-3691
San Diego (619) 463-9275
San Francisco/Oakland
(510) 568-9214

## COLORADO
**Combined Charity Services of Colorado**
1311 W. Alameda Avenue
Denver, CO  80223
(303) 777-8676

**Metro Volunteers**
1600 Sherman Street
Denver, CO  80203
(303) 894-0103

**Junior Achievement**
One Education Way
Colorado Springs, CO
80906-4477
(719) 540-8000

**Volunteer Connection**
584 Mohawk Drive
Boulder, CO  80303
(303) 444-4904

**Volunteers of America**
Denver (303) 297-0408

**Windstar Foundation**
2317 Snowmass Creek Road
Snowmass, CO 81654
(303) 927-4777
(303) 927-4778

## CONNECTICUT
**AmeriCares Foundation**
161 Cherry Street
New Canaan, CT 06840
(203) 966-5195

**Friends of Animals**
777 Post Road, Suite 205
Darien, CT 06820
(203) 866-5223

## DELAWARE
**Girls Inc. of Delaware**
3301 Green Street
Claymont, DE
19703-2062
(302) 798-9243

**Volunteers for Adolescent Pregnancy Prevention**
611 W. 18th Street
Wilmington, DE
19802-4707
(302) 658-3331

## DISTRICT OF COLUMBIA
**American Association of Retired Persons (AARP)**
1909 K Street NW
Washington, DC 20049
(202) 662-4895

**American Red Cross**
431 18th Street NW
Washington, DC 20006
(202) 737-8300

**B'nai B'rith Youth Organization**
1640 Rhode Island Avenue NW
Washington, DC 20036
(202) 857-6633

**City Cares of America**
1737 H Street NW
Washington, DC 20006
(202) 887-0500

**Greenpeace U.S.A.**
1432 U Street NW
Washington, DC 20009
(202) 462-1177

**Keyette International**
1421 Kalmia Road NW
Washington, DC 20012
(202) 726-4619

Points of Light
Foundation
1737 H Street NW
Washington, DC 20006
(202) 223-9186
(800) 879-5400

Witness for Peace
110 Maryland Avenue NE,
No. 311
Washington, DC 20002
(202) 544-0781

Youth Service America
1101 15th Street NW,
Suite 200
Washington, DC 20005
(202) 296-2992

**FLORIDA**
Food for the Poor
1301 W. Copans Road
Pompano Beach, FL
33064
(305) 975-0000

Hands on Miami
1 S.E. 3rd Ave, Suite 2000
Miami, FL 33131
(305) 579-2300

Junior Chamber
International
400 University Drive
Coral Gables, FL 33134
(305) 446-7608

Volunteers of America
Tampa/St. Petersburg
(813) 282-1525

**GEORGIA**
Boys and Girls Clubs of
America
1230 West Peachtree Street
Atlanta, GA 30309
(404) 815-5700

Habitat for Humanity
121 Habitat Street
Americus, GA
31709-3498
(912) 924-6935

Pilot International
244 College Street
P.O. Box 4844
Macon, GA 31213-0599
(912) 743-7403

**HAWAII**
Pacific Whale Foundation
Kealia Beach Plaza,
Suite 25
101 N. Kihei Road
Kihei, HI 96753
(808) 879-8811

Teenage Assembly of
America
441 Mananai Place No. E
Honolulu, HI 96818
(808) 486-5959

**IDAHO**
Peregrine Fund
World Center for Birds of
Prey
5666 W. Flying Hawk Lane
Boise, ID 83709
(208) 362-3716

**ILLINOIS**
Little Brothers—Friends
of the Elderly
1658 W. Belmont Avenue
Chicago, IL 60657
(312) 477-7702

National Children's
Cancer Society
3 Sunset Hills Executive
Park, Suite 4
Edwardsville, IL 62205
(618) 882-6227

Ronald McDonald
Children's Charities
1 Kroc Drive
Oak Brook, IL 60521
(708) 575-3000

Volunteers of America
Chicago (312) 707-8707

**Young Men's Christian Associations of the U.S.A. (YMCA U.S.A.)**
101 N. Wacker Drive
Chicago, IL 60606
(312) 977-0031

## INDIANA
**Key Club**
3636 Woodview Trace
Indianapolis, IN
46268-3196
(317) 875-8755

**Kiwanis International**
3636 Woodview Trace
Indianapolis, IN
46268-3196
(317) 875-8755
(800) 549-2647

**Volunteers of America**
Indianapolis
(317) 686-5800

## IOWA
**Special Recreation**
362 Koser Avenue
Iowa City, IA 52246-3038
(319) 337-7578

**Indian Youth of America**
609 Badgerow Building
P.O. Box 2786
Sioux City, IA 51106
(712) 252-3230

## KANSAS
**La Sertoma International**
12612 W. 101st Street
Lenexa, KS 66215
(913) 492-3116

**Youth Volunteer Corps of America**
6310 Lamar Avenue,
Suite 125
Overland Park, KS 66202
(913) 423-9822

## KENTUCKY
**The Dream Factory**
P.O. Box 3942
Louisville, KY
40201-3942
(502) 584-3928
(800) 456-7556

**Volunteers of America**
Louisville (502) 636-0771
Lexington (606) 254-3467

## LOUISIANA
**Volunteers of America**
(national headquarters)
3939 N. Causeway
Boulevard
Metairie, LA 70002
(504) 837-2652
(800) 899-0089

**Volunteers of America**
Baton Rouge
(504) 387-0061
New Orleans
(504) 836-5225
Shreveport
(318) 221-2669

## MAINE
**Samantha Smith Center**
9 Union Street
Hallowell, ME 04347
(207) 626-3415

**Volunteers of America**
Portland (207) 871-7174

## MARYLAND
**American Rescue Workers**
716 Ritchie Road
Capital Heights, MD
20743
(301) 336-6200

**Activism 2000 Project**
P.O. Box E
Kensington, MD 20895
(301) 929-8808
1-800-KID-POWER

**Goodwill Industries of America**
9200 Wisconsin Avenue
Bethesda, MD 20814
(310) 530-6500

**Volunteers of America**
Baltimore (301) 459-2020

## MASSACHUSETTS
**Grassroots International**
48 Grove Street No. 103
Somerville, MA 02144
(617) 628-1664

**International Wildlife Coalition**
70 E. Falmouth Highway
Box 388
East Falmouth, MA 02536
(508) 548-8328

**A School for Iqbal Fund**
Hibernia Savings Bank
731 Hancock Street
Quincy, MA 02170
http://www.digitalrag.com/mirror/iqbal.html

**Volunteers of America**
Boston (617) 522-8086

## MICHIGAN
**Good Fellows (Old Newsboys)**
P.O. Box 32702
Detroit, MI 48232
(313) 961-3355

**Volunteer Impact** (Detroit)
23077 Greenfield Road, Suite LL10
Southfield, MI 48075
(810) 559-4950

**Volunteers of America**
Detroit (810) 548-4090
Lansing (517) 484-4414

## MINNESOTA
**A Chance to Grow**
5034 Oliver Avenue N
Minneapolis, MN 55430
(612) 521-2266

**National Youth Leadership Council**
1910 West County Road B
Roseville, MN 55113
(612) 631-3672

**Volunteers of America**
Minneapolis/St. Paul
(612) 546-3242

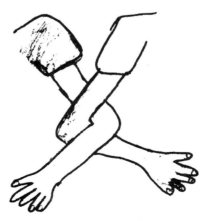

## MISSISSIPPI
**Greater Jackson Youth Service Corps**
c/o George Jackson
517 N. Farish Street
Jackson, MS 39202-3202
(601) 353-1311

## MISSOURI
**Camp Fire Boys and Girls**
4601 Madison Avenue
Kansas City, MO 64112
(816) 756-1950

**Earth Angels**
P.O. Box 2055
St. Louis, MO 63158
(314) 231-3188

**Junior Optimist Clubs**
4494 Lindell Boulevard
St. Louis, MO 63108
(314) 371-6000

## MONTANA
**Crimestoppers of Helena**
P.O. Box 1212
Helena, MT 59624-1212
(406) 442-5820

**Montana Communities in Action for a Drug Free Youth, Inc.**
c/o Mamie Flinn
P.O. Box 332
Helena, MT 59624-0332
(406) 443-7110

**Tots, Toys, and Tales, Inc.**
c/o Denise Herman
P.O. Box 221
Harlowton, MT
59036-0221
(406) 632-5550

## NEBRASKA
**National Arbor Day Foundation**
100 Arbor Avenue
Nebraska City, NE 68410
(402) 474-5655

**Volunteers of America**
Lewellen (308) 778-5548

## NEVADA
**Food for Kids, Inc.**
4820 Alpine Place,
Suite H201
Las Vegas, NV
89107-4080
(702) 877-5437

**Volunteers of America**
Reno (702) 825-8400

## NEW HAMPSHIRE
**Earth Day U.S.A.**
P.O. Box 470
Peterborough, NH 03458
(603) 924-7720

**Soldiers for Peace**
46 Union Street
Peterborough, NH 03458
(603) 924-6811

## NEW JERSEY
**Jersey Cares**
330 South Street
Morristown, NJ 07960
(201) 644-4952

**Volunteers of America**
Trenton/Camden/
Southern New Jersey
(609) 854-4660
Bergen County/
Northern New Jersey
(212) 873-2600

## NEW MEXICO
**Futures for Children**
805 Tijeras NW
Albuquerque, NM 87102
(505) 247-4700

**St. Jude Express**
P.O. Box 5333
Albuquerque, NM 87185
(505) 268-5051

## NEW YORK
**Friendship Ambassadors Foundation**
40 Waller Avenue
White Plains, NY 10601
(914) 328-8589

**Girl Scouts of the U.S.A.**
420 5th Avenue
New York, NY 10018
(212) 852-8000

**Girls Inc.**
30 E. 33rd Street
New York, NY 10016
(212) 689-3700

**Kids STOP**
P.O. Box 750471
Forest Hills, NY
11375-0471

**National Jewish Girl Scout Committee**
33 Central Drive
Bronxville, NY 10708
(914) 738-3986

**United Nations Children's Fund (UNICEF)**
3 United Nations Plaza
New York, NY 10017
(212) 326-7000
(212) 702-7100

**Volunteers of America**
NYC/Westchester
(212) 873-2600
Rochester/Western
New York
(716) 454-1150

**United Synagogue Youth**
155 Fifth Avenue
New York, NY 10010
(212) 533-7800

Young Judea
50 W. 58th Street
New York, NY 10019
(212) 303-4575

**NORTH CAROLINA**
Hands on Charlotte
1616 Central Avenue,
Suite 200
Charlotte, NC 28205
(704) 333-7471

**NORTH DAKOTA**
Bismarck Emergency
Food Pantry
207 E. Front Avenue,
Room B
Bismarck, ND
58504-5511
(701) 258-9188

Lakota Community Club
c/o Bruce Anderson
P.O. Box 505
Lakota, ND 58344-0505
(701) 247-2482

**OHIO**
Free Store/Food Bank
112 E. Liberty Street
Cincinnati, OH 45210
(513) 241-1064

Good Bears of the World
P.O. Box 13097
Toledo, OH 43613
(419) 531-5365

Volunteers of America
Cincinnati
(513) 381-1954
Cleveland (216) 621-1738
Columbus/Dayton
(614) 224-8650
Mansfield (419) 525-4589
Sandusky (419) 626-6505
Toledo (419) 248-3733

**OKLAHOMA**
World Neighbors
4127 N.W. 122 Street
Oklahoma City, OK
73120-9933
(405) 752-9700

Volunteers of America
Tulsa (918) 663-1153

**OREGON**
Hands on Portland
P.O. Box 4922
Portland , OR 97208
(503) 222-3331

Holt International
Children's Services
P.O. Box 2880
Eugene, OR 97402
(541) 687-2202

Volunteers of America
Portland (503) 235-8655

**PENNSYLVANIA**
Big Brothers/Big Sisters of
America
230 N. 13th Street
Philadelphia, PA 19107
(215) 567-7000

NGA, Inc.
1007-B Street Road
Southampton, PA 18966
(215) 322-5759

Soroptimist International
of the Americas
1616 Walnut Street,
Suite 700
Philadelphia, PA 19103
(215) 732-0512

Volunteers of America
Allentown/Bethlehem
(610) 432-8352
Harrisburg/Lancaster/York
(717) 236-1440
Philadelphia
(609) 854-4660
Wilkes Barre/Scranton
(717) 825-5261

## RHODE ISLAND
**Plan International U.S.A.**
P.O. Box 7670
Warwick, RI 02887
(401) 294-3693

**Volunteers in Action, Inc.**
168 Broad Street
Providence, RI
02903-4028
(401) 421-6547

## SOUTH CAROLINA
**Hands on Greenville**
P.O. Box 9072
Greenville, SC 29604
(864) 242-4224

**Volunteers of America**
Charleston/Columbia
(803) 779-6465

## SOUTH DAKOTA
**Crippled Children's
Foundation**
2501 W. 26th Street
Sioux Falls, SD
57105-2446
(605) 336-1840

**Volunteers of America**
Sioux Falls
(605) 338-3461

## TENNESSEE
**Hands on Nashville**
P.O. Box 120615
Nashville, TN 37212
(615) 298-1108

**KIDS FACE (Kids for a
Clean Environment)**
P.O. Box 158254
Nashville, TN 37215
(800) 952-3223

**Volunteers of America**
Knoxville (423) 525-7136

## TEXAS
**Association for Retarded
Citizens (ARC)**
500 E. Border Street,
Suite 300
Arlington, TX 76010
(817) 261-6003

**Boy Scouts of America**
1325 West Walnut Hill
Lane
P.O. Box 152079
Irving, TX 75015
(214) 580-2000

**Volunteers of America**
Dallas/Fort Worth
(817) 649-7491
Houston (713) 956-6310

## UTAH
**Children's Miracle
Network**
7106 South Highland
Drive
Salt Lake City, UT 84121
(801) 942-2200

**Volunteers of America**
Salt Lake City
(801) 363-9414

## VERMONT
**Community Action
Brattleboro Area, Inc.**
53 Frost Street
Brattleboro, VT
05301-3226
(802) 257-7051

**Volunteers for Peace**
43 Tiffany Road
Belmont, VT 05730
(802) 259-2759

## VIRGINIA
**Children, Inc.**
P.O. Box 5381
1000 Westover Road
Richmond, VA 23220
(804) 359-4562
(800) 538-5381

**Gifts in Kind America**
700 N. Fairfax Street,
Suite 300
Alexandria, VA 22314
(703) 836-2121

**Salvation Army**
National Headquarters
615 Slaters Lane
P.O. Box 269
Alexandria, VA 22313
(703) 684-5500

**United Way of America**
701 N. Fairfax Street
Alexandria, VA
22314-2045
(703) 836-7100

## WASHINGTON
**The Benefit Gang**
P.O. Box 1989
Seattle, WA 98111-1989
(206) 443-3277

**Childcare International**
1310 Broadway
Bellingham, WA 98225
(206) 647-2283

**Giraffe Project**
197 Second Street
P.O. Box 759
Langley, WA 98260
(206) 221-7989

**Volunteers of America**
Everett/Northwest
(206) 259-3191
Seattle/Tacoma
(206) 523-3565
Spokane (509) 624-2378

## WASHINGTON, D.C. (see DISTRICT OF COLUMBIA)

## WEST VIRGINIA
**Center for New National Security**
P.O. Box 444
Bakerton, WV 25410
(304) 876-9400

**United Community Services, Inc.**
133 5th Avenue
Montgomery, WV
25136-2229
(304) 442-5177

## WISCONSIN
**Family Service America**
11700 W. Lake Park Drive
Milwaukee, WI 53224
(414) 359-1040

**Volunteers of America**
Milwaukee
(414) 896-3611

## WYOMING
**Volunteers of America**
Sheridan (307) 672-0475

# AUTHORS AND TEACHERS

## FOURTH GRADE
### Westridge Elementary
*wrote about Jim Stuart
Runner-Beuning*
Carolyn Doggett and Wendy
Riddle, Teachers

Sonja Marie Acker
Matthew Bosick
Nicole L. Brown
Sarah Donnelly
Olivia Dudley
Sara Evans
Benae Lisa Esquibel
Jenna Gregg
Ben Robert Herodes
Matt Knutson
Ike Morrow
Zach Morse
Cody Parker
Melissa A. Peterson
Shawn Michael Phelan
Stephanie N. Powers
Corinthea Procopis
Danielle Quintana
Jessica C. Rombough
Eric Sabin
Travis V. Sabin
Eric Seagren

Amanda J. Stowe
Randi Sugar
Valerie Swigert
Chad Towner
Robert Vroman
Brittany Walters
Dylan Williams
Adam Wolff

*Westridge fourth grade (Huggins/Riddle)*

## FOURTH GRADE
### Westridge Elementary
*wrote about Christy Surrency*
Samantha Huggins and Wendy
Riddle, Teachers

Sean Allison
Aaron Arguello
Monica J. Atencio
Erin Becker
Paul Michael Berens
Jessica M. Cruz
Elizabeth M. Dolif
D. J. Donizio
Theodora Dryer
Brandice R. Edwards
Thomas E. Frank
Stephanie Gorton
Troy Grim
Jerad M. Linder
Nicole Miller
Scott C. Miller

*Westridge fourth grade (Doggett/Riddle)*

Christopher W. Mitchell
Michael Lynn Neyman
Emily A. Peconi
Stephanie Marie Potter
Matt Schambow
Shannon J. Schupbach
Crista Shuman
Erik Skinner
Zach Stewart
Emily Thornton
Tony Vigil
Rachel Ann White

## WESTRIDGE ELEMENTARY WRITING CLUB

*wrote about Renata Bradford,
Teddy Andrews, Emily Greble,
Brianne Schwantes, David Levitt,
and Ashley Black*
Jeannie Cable, Teacher

Paul M. Berens
Adam Brown
Neal M. Campbell
Nathan Christensen
Katie Farnum
Desirae Ford
Brittany Gardner

*Peiffer fifth grade*

Callie B. Kendrick
Caitlin McGann
Eric W. Meldrum
Tony Milano
Chrissi Moorman
Kathryn C. Overturf
Ashley Redd
Brendan Riddle
Alissa Smith

Amanda J. Stowe
Sara Tafoya
Melissa VanDonkelaar
Laura Vroman

## FIFTH GRADE
### Peiffer Elementary

*wrote about Charlie Wolfe*
Edith Glapion, Jeannie Cable,
and Wendy Riddle, Teachers

Brent Anderson
Cameron Anderson
Stephanie L. Beckham
J. M. Belk
Vanessa Butrum
Danielle Cook
Shawn Elliott
Daniel S. Janes Jr.
Sarah Jenkins
Caleb Joseph Kolenc
Zandria Lane
Kevin Magee
Carolyn Marsh
Michael Martinez
Victoria Myers

*Westridge Writing Club*

Daniel Packard
Jessica Padgett
Steven Reilly
Kristina Russell
Lauren Salmon
Wayde James Samuel
Staci Slatkavitz
Christopher J. Smith
Kara Whitelock
Jeffrey Wingfield

*Deer Creek Writing Club*

## COMBINED THIRD, FOURTH, AND FIFTH GRADE
### Columbine Elementary
*wrote about Twyla Rivers*
Mae Davies, Susan Holmes, and Shirley Merdes, Teachers

Sierra Armstrong
Julienne Bemski
Lauren Black
Jason Carey
Mark C. Fimberg
Joe Ford
Jerry J. Garcia
Emma G. Grant
Heidi M. Homburger
Tenishia Jones
Billy McCarren
Edward Mutegi
Rozelia Nelson

Genevieve Nuebel
Sydney H. Park
Ian Addison Philipp
David W. Rector
James G. Rector
Twyla Rivers
Sahada Sesay
Aysha K. Shehim
Veronica Wylie

## DEER CREEK MIDDLE SCHOOL WRITING CLUB
*wrote about Michael Crisler and Sarah Swagart*
Eileen Carlston, Teacher

Bryan Attardi
Ben Bergman
Angela Bevis
Kitty Carlston
Ben Carvalho
Brandon Champlin
Sarah Cherrington
Andrea Cooley
Greg Cross
Brian Favier
Nicole Grahm
Ryan Hanlon
Angela Hendricks
Jessica Johnson
Jennifer Kircher
Julius Lee
Jackie McOmber
Liz Mortimer
Tara Myers
Cari Rons
Vanessa Salazar
Jason Silvanage
Wade Stern
Jesse Stone
Rob Thelen
Cliff Ward
Ben Winkler
Lindsey Winters

*Columbine combined class*

## SIXTH GRADE
### Wilmore Davis Elementary
*wrote about Kory Johnson, Iqbal Masih, Edward Santos, and Iqbal's Friends in Quincy*
Jeannie Cable, Teacher

Briana Anderson
Sarah Andrews
Nicole Aragon
Adrian G. Chidester
Brittany Curtis
Jimmy A. Garcia
Eric Gonzales
Jerrod Kay
Tyler David Lutz
Anatoly Matveyuk
Ryan McLaughlin
Jeff Near
Christopher Paulson
Matt Quinlan
Jenny Reaney
Donald Reisbeck
Lauren Schmidt
Kristina Smedberg
Pamela Marie Stigall
Eric Van Bourgondien
Shannon Weakland
Scott (Dyck) Weise
Annie Wilson

## FOURTH GRADE
### Prospect Valley Elementary
*wrote about Melissa Poe and Cari Rons*
Pat Rhodes, Teacher

Scott Andrews
Tiffany Bradford
Jenna Buschkoetter
Erica Clark
Melody Coleman

*Prospect Valley fourth grade*

Sarah DeLeo
Lee A. DeRose
Jeannine DiCarlantonio
Emily Freeman
Alissa Dawn Harvey
Will Hollingsworth
Alyssa James
Brad Koniz
Justin Linenberger
Christopher J. May
Sarah McNerney
Molly Norris
Benjamin M. Owens
Alex Polesovsky

Jessica Rodrigues
Garin Runyon
Scott Glenn Selby
Mitchell Sigg
Efraim Silva
Grant Kiel Stoneking
Cameran Taton

## OTHER CONTRIBUTORS:
Jeannie Cable, Codirector
Judith H. Cozzens, Consultant
Melissa R. Lobach, Director
Wendy Riddle, Codirector

*Wilmore Davis sixth grade*

# INDEX

### American Origins Series

Each is 48 pages and $12.95 hardcover.
**Tracing Our English Roots**
**Tracing Our German Roots**
**Tracing Our Irish Roots**
**Tracing Our Italian Roots**
**Tracing Our Japanese Roots**
**Tracing Our Jewish Roots**
**Tracing Our Polish Roots**

### Bizarre & Beautiful Series

Each is 48 pages, $14.95 hardcover, $9.95 paperback.
**Bizarre & Beautiful Ears**
**Bizarre & Beautiful Eyes**
**Bizarre & Beautiful Feelers**
**Bizarre & Beautiful Noses**
**Bizarre & Beautiful Tongues**

### Extremely Weird® Series

Each is 32 pages and $5.95 paperback.
**Extremely Weird Animal Defenses**
**Extremely Weird Animal Disguises**
**Extremely Weird Animal Hunters**
**Extremely Weird Bats**
**Extremely Weird Endangered Species**
**Extremely Weird Fishes**
**Extremely Weird Frogs**
**Extremely Weird Reptiles**
**Extremely Weird Spiders**
**Extremely Weird Birds**
**Extremely Weird Insects**
**Extremely Weird Mammals**
**Extremely Weird Micro Monsters**
**Extremely Weird Primates**
**Extremely Weird Sea Creatures**
**Extremely Weird Snakes**

### Kidding Around® Travel Series

Each is 144 pages and $7.95 paperback.
**Kidding Around Atlanta**
**Kidding Around Austin** (9/97)
**Kidding Around Boston** (9/97)
**Kidding Around Cleveland**
**Kids Go! Denver**
**Kidding Around Indianapolis**
**Kidding Around Kansas City**
**Kidding Around Miami** (10/97)
**Kidding Around Milwaukee** (9/97)
**Kidding Around Minneapolis/St. Paul**
**Kidding Around San Francisco**
**Kids Go! Seattle**
**Kidding Around Washington, D.C.**

### Kids Explore Series

Written by kids for kids, each is $9.95 paperback.
**Kids Explore America's African American Heritage**, 160 pages
**Kids Explore America's Hispanic Heritage**, 160 pages
**Kids Explore America's Japanese American Heritage**, 160 pages
**Kids Explore America's Jewish Heritage**, 160 pages
**Kids Explore the Gifts of Children with Special Needs**, 128 pages
**Kids Explore the Heritage of Western Native Americans**, 128 pages

### Rough and Ready Series

Each is 48 pages and $4.95 paperback.
**Rough and Ready Homesteaders**
**Rough and Ready Cowboys**
**Rough and Ready Loggers**
**Rough and Ready Outlaws and Lawmen**
**Rough and Ready Prospectors**
**Rough and Ready Railroaders**

### X-ray Vision Series

Each is 48 pages and $6.95 paperback.
**Looking Inside the Brain**
**Looking Inside Cartoon Animation**
**Looking Inside Caves and Caverns**
**Looking Inside Sports Aerodynamics**
**Looking Inside Sunken Treasure**
**Looking Inside Telescopes and the Night Sky**

### Ordering Information

Please check your local bookstore for our books, or call **1-800-888-7504** to order direct and to receive a complete catalog. A shipping charge will be added to your order total.

Send all inquiries to:
**John Muir Publications
P.O. Box 613, Santa Fe, NM 87504**